WHAT I HEARD

**My Conversations with
Slavoj Žižek
Mahathir Mohamad
Vijay Prashad
Rhodri Jeffreys-Jones
Sivaraman Ramanathan, Et al**

***

NILANTHA ILANGAMUWA

To Parents
For Everything

I Think; Therefore, I Am ~ **René Descartes**

The First Duty of Love is to Listen ~ **Paul Tillich**

CONTENTS

FOREWORD

"What I Heard" is a collection of insights gathered from distinguished voices of our time, reflecting a collective will to embrace the diverse echoes that resonate across various media platforms. This publication seeks to weave a tapestry of perspectives, drawing from the intellectual realms of luminaries such as Slavoj Žižek, Vijay Prashad, and the influential political landscapes shaped by figures like Mahathir Mohamad, Rhodri Jeffries-Jones, Sivarama Ramanathan, Dayan Jayatilleka, and Ali Sabry.

These discussions serve as windows flung wide open into the very essence of our shared human experience. "What I Heard" does more than capture the spirit of our age; it resounds with the urgency of a world where ideas collide, perspectives clash, and the echoes of intellectual discourse cascade like a torrent. It is not just a collection of voices; it is a symphony, with each interview recording a unique reflection of the myriad chords that compose our global discourse. Through these conversations, I attempt to delve into answers for some of our fundamental questions, break down the complexities of politics, and navigate the interplay between ideology and reality.

The richness and depth of the insights presented in this book highlight the diverse perspectives contributed by diplomats and esteemed figures. Muhammad Saad Khattak, the former Pakistan High Commissioner to Sri Lanka, along with Demet Şekercioğlu, the Ambassador of the Republic of Turkey to Sri Lanka, and Tareq Md Ariful Islam, the High Commissioner of Bangladesh to Sri Lanka, have collectively enhanced the content with their diplomatic wisdom. Furthermore, the inclusion of voices from the realm of higher education in Sri Lanka, such as Sampath Amaratunga, the former Vice-Chancellor of Sri Jayewardenepura University and Chairman of the University Grants Commission, as well as Sivakolundu

Srisatkunarajah, a distinguished Professor in Mathematics and Vice-Chancellor of the University of Jaffna, adds a valuable academic perspective to the narrative.

The selection of 25 interviews from numerous conducted over the past few years aims to capture diverse perspectives from various walks of society. This selection strives to provide a representative understanding of different fields and communities.

Let me thank all those who shared their thoughts, making this book possible. Their valuable contributions have enriched the depth and breadth of this work. However, it is essential to note that the opinions expressed within these pages belong to the respective contributors and do not necessarily reflect the views of the author or the publisher.

January 2024
Colombo, Sri Lanka

INTRODUCTION

*Where you will sit when you are old, shows where you stood in youth. ~ **Yoruba Proverb***

*The art of conversation lies in listening. ~ **Malcolm Forbes***

MEMORY is the very foundation of culture. Devoid of memory, civilisation crumbles, society dissipates, the future becomes an abyss, and the nation-state loses its essence. No external force can vanquish a great civilisation unless it first succumbs to internal decay and self-destruction. As Sigmund Freud noted, *Civilisation began the first time an angry man replaced a stone with a word.* The essential product of words is dialogue. Conversations are the backbone of human civilisation. The gathering of other people who are curious to hear someone's story can be called the beginning of a community. It is no exaggeration to say that it extended from the tribes to the creation of the nation-state. As Martin Heidegger noted, *we, mandkind, are a conversation.* The content and context of conversations are the driving force of human civilisation. It is a sign of social degradation as well as decadence.

Ancient sources, such as texts, inscriptions, and manuscripts, provide basic information about historical events, cultures, and societies. Conversations in these sources can provide insight into the thoughts, beliefs, and perspectives of individuals from different periods. Also, dialogues in ancient sources help us understand the cultural context of a particular era. They provide information about social norms, customs, language use, and everyday life, contributing to a more comprehensive understanding of a civilisation. Meanwhile, many ancient conversations come from philosophical and intellectual traditions. The works of ancient philosophers such as Plato or Aristotle form the basis of Western philosophy. Studying these conversations allows us to grasp the origins of philosophical ideas and trace the development of intellectual thought.

Dialogues in ancient literature, such as dramas, epics, and poems, are valuable for literary analysis. Examining dialogue structure and character interactions can reveal themes, symbolism, and narrative techniques used by ancient writers. Ancient legal and political writings, meanwhile, often include dialogues that shed light on systems of governance, legal codes, and political structures of the time. These sources help to understand the foundations of modern political systems and legal principles.

Also, many ancient religious texts and mythological stories are presented in the form of dialogues. These dialogues provide insight into the spiritual beliefs, rituals, and moral codes of ancient societies and provide the basis for various religious traditions. Moreover, one of the most important things is that the study of dialogues from ancient sources helps to understand the evolution of languages. Changes in vocabulary, grammar, and linguistic expressions over time can be traced through these texts.

These conversations serve as a means of preserving knowledge. Without these written records, we would lose much of the wisdom, ideas, and experiences of ancient civilisations. Therefore, conducting conversations as well as documenting them can be said to be a habit that began in history. In its ability to act as a window into the past, providing a rich understanding of the history, culture, philosophy, literature, law, religion, and language of the human journey. It allows us to connect with the thoughts and conversations of people who lived in different times, enriching our appreciation of the diversity of human experience through the ages.

In Plato's Apology, when he asked Socrates what his definition of wisdom was, Socrates replied, "The only true wisdom is knowing that you know nothing." The intrinsic value of a conversation is its human excitement. According to The Analects of Confucius, one of his disciples, Zilu, asks him about the nature of goodness. Confucius said, "To be able to practice five things everywhere under heaven constitutes perfect virtue: gravity, generosity of soul, sincerity, earnestness, and kindness. If you can practice these, you can be called a good man." In the Dhammachakkappavattana Sutra, when asked what is the cause of suffering, Gautama Buddha preached, "Greed is the cause of suffering."

In the dialogue between Enkidu and Shamhat in the epic of Gilgamesh, from ancient Mesopotamia, who was wise in all matters? When asked, "who saw the depth, the foundation of the country, who knew...", is said to have replied. Also, for Arjuna, according to the Bhagavad Gita, what is the correct approach to action? When asked, Krishna is said to have replied, "You have a right to perform your prescribed duties, but you have no right to the fruits of your actions." Our history is full of such conversations.

An indispensable facet of journalism lies in its profound ability to traverse diverse disciplines, fostering an environment that encourages open dialogue with individuals from various walks of life. Journalists, as conduits of information, possess the unique skill to engage with people across different fields and create a space where conversations unfold freely. This entails the capacity to approach narratives without preconceived notions or biases, allowing for an authentic exploration of the perspectives, experiences, and insights that individuals bring to the table. In the journalistic endeavour to uncover and share stories, the art of unbiased listening becomes paramount, enabling the profession to serve as a bridge between disparate worlds, ultimately contributing to a more comprehensive and nuanced understanding of the complex tapestry of human experiences.

I talked to people, anyone I thought, that they would like to share their thoughts. Moreover, as I always believe in the old saying "everyone has a story", I like to listen to their stories, and I added "their stories are much greater than mine". Becoming a journalist was a fluke, so when my parents saw that my political commentators were being published in the mainstream media, there were disputes at home. Sometimes, like others of their generation, they live in deep-seated trauma due to the country's violent history.

Regrettably, in the aftermath of a wounded generation, the pivotal task of constructing meaningful connections between the scars of the past and the succeeding generation has been grievously neglected. The failure to socially reengineer these constructive dialogues has left a conspicuous lacuna of confusion, enabling the seeds of insecurity to permeate reality. While some societies around the world have endeavoured to heal the wounds inflicted by a series of shocking events through connectivity, Sri Lanka remains entangled in the unresolved matter of addressing this crucial need. The imperative of forging a path towards understanding and unity is undeniable, and until this profound responsibility is acknowledged and embraced, the echoes of insecurity will persist, hindering the collective progress towards reconciliation and resilience.

From ancient history to the present day, questions and answers in conversation are like the relationship between body and blood. Conversation is the main tool used to communicate one person to another group and person to person. It is the heartbeat of understanding, the pulse of shared knowledge, and the lifeline of our collective human experience.

Allow me to draw your attention to two pivotal conversations in political history, among the millions that exist. Each serves as a testimony to the power of dialogue and represents the unique challenges of the era in which they unfolded. First, consider the correspondence between Abraham Lincoln and Frederick Douglass. Born in a humble log cabin in Kentucky to illiterate parents, Lincoln's thirst for knowledge drove him to self-education. In stark contrast, Douglass, a former slave, understood the connection between literacy and freedom at an early age. Despite his circumstances, he taught himself to read and write, with his education culminating in the creation of a revolutionary book, *'The Columbian Orator.'*

During the Civil War, Lincoln and Douglass engaged in a correspondence that echoed the profound struggle for freedom. Douglass, a leading abolitionist, implored Lincoln to permit African Americans to join the Union Army, underscoring their commitment to the cause.

A second compelling example is found in the exchanges between John F. Kennedy and Nikita Khrushchev during the Cuban Missile Crisis. Faced with the threat of catastrophic conflict, the leaders' dialogue, including letters and telegrams, proved instrumental in diffusing tensions and averting war.

The occurrence of these two incidents, in my perspective, exemplifies the remarkable qualities inherent in humanity. It underscores the transformative power of dialogue, demonstrating that individuals from vastly different socio-economic backgrounds and belief systems can converge through mutual understanding. This convergence, fueled by open conversation, holds the potential to resolve even the most perilous crises. These occurrences serve as a clear affirmation to the capacity of shared dialogue to bridge divides, fostering unity among people who, on the surface, may appear worlds apart. Such instances of harmonious interaction offer a beacon of hope, illustrating that, despite our differences, the shared threads of empathy and understanding can weave a fabric that binds us together, transcending the barriers that often seem insurmountable.

However, the current global political landscape demands a rekindling of dialogue. The clash between the unipolar and multipolar world orders, coupled with escalating social tensions, calls for renewed and disciplined conversation. In a world where power-driven abuses overshadow sacrifices for peace, disciplined dialogue becomes imperative. It offers a pathway to mutual respect and understanding, transcending narrow political interests. In the face of existing challenges, it stands as the sole method for resolution.

Currently, the world is contending with more than 30 armed conflicts, each stemming from diverse political issues. Bloodshed spans continents, displacing countless lives daily. Despite discussions on peace, the dream of conflict resolution remains elusive. It exposes the paradox of human civilization— we talk of peace, yet engage in more wars. It mirrors our approach to freedom, an undefined ideal we strive to interpret individually. In the words of Slavoj Žižek, *'freedom is an incurable disease,'* underscoring the enigma of our relentless pursuit amid perpetual conflict. The urgency for dialogue has never been more pressing.

In this pivotal context, I deemed it paramount to disseminate the profound ideas of a select few among the myriad individuals I've had the privilege to interview in recent years. While several of these conversations found their way into various newspapers, the significance of consolidating them into a singular volume became evident. The culmination of insights, perspectives, and narratives, now encapsulated in a book, stands as a monument to the collective wisdom drawn from diverse voices.

The realisation of this endeavour was made possible by the generous support of a multitude of individuals, both local and international journalists, who lent their assistance in conducting these interviews. While their names may not all find mention here, I seize this moment to extend my deepest gratitude to each and every one of them. However, I wish to express my sincere appreciation to at least a few of those whose support has significantly influenced my work; I feel it is unjust not to mention them. I extend my deepest thanks to esteemed editors from respected publications, including Manik De Silva of Sunday Island, Nisthar Cassim of DailyFT, Gyaneshwar Dayal of Daily Pioneer, and Jeffrey St Clair of Counterpunch. Their belief in my writings and steadfast commitment to their publication over the past few years have provided immense encouragement. Gratitude is also due to my wife, Bhabani Sonowal, and her colleagues—Chandrika Mehta, Avnish Singh, Pooja Raghav, Preeti Singh, Trishna Rai, Sibaram Badatya, and Naveen Gautam—for being resolute pillars of support. I am equally indebted to journalists and foreign service professionals in their respective countries, including Tomasz Augustyniak, Ayanjit Sen, Ivin Alexandr Viktorovich, Mostafa Hashemi, Oleh Hulak, and Goolbai Gunasekara. Special acknowledgment goes to my relatives, Muskan Sonowal and Kapil Sharma. It is indeed a privilege to be surrounded by remarkable colleagues and friends, including Anver Hamdani, Jeevanthie Senanayake, Rukshana Rizwie, Dinushika Thamali Perera, Kanchana Gayani Rajapaksha, Manoj Munasinghe, Prabhath Senanayake, Chamara Deepal, and Mahalingam Arulkumaran whose collective presence has enriched both my professional and personal journey. Their collaboration has been instrumental, breathing life into these conversations and contributing to the realisation of this impactful compilation.

We are living in an interesting era dominated by artificial intelligence. Journalism is undergoing a profound transformation with the rise of AI-Journalism. This evolving paradigm is compelling newsrooms to undergo extensive overhauls, adapting to the rapid pace at which the world of AI progresses. Even seasoned practitioners find it challenging to keep abreast of the latest developments, making it imperative to explore recent changes in AI technology and discern trends relevant to journalism.

The urgency surrounding strategic communication about AI in

news organizations stems from the widespread awareness among individuals associated with these entities regarding the capabilities of AI tools and their potential for significant disruption. Practitioners within the news industry are already immersed in experimenting with these tools, scrutinizing reports, evaluating potential applications, and posing critical questions. While the ideal scenario would involve a patient assessment followed by a meticulously devised strategy, such luxury may not be viable given the rapid evolution of AI.

Therefore, a more practical communication strategy entails acknowledging the situation, articulating the organization's engagement with and learning about AI, and providing clear guidelines for its early or limited use. The emphasis should be on demonstrating innovative approaches, signaling adaptability, and preparing for the inevitable changes that lie ahead. Importantly, maintaining a tone of optimism and excitement for AI's potential to elevate journalism beyond mere information dissemination, making it more accessible to a broader audience, is essential.

In journalism, the paramount concern is safeguarding the originality of sources, as it is this authenticity that forms the bedrock of credibility in content. As we navigate the intersection of AI and journalism, the focus remains on preserving the integrity and uniqueness of sources, ensuring that journalistic principles are upheld, and leveraging AI as a tool to enhance, rather than compromise, the quality and accessibility of news. Whether we like it or not, technological advancements, from algorithms to artificial intelligence, are an undeniable reality. However, interpersonal conversations will remain pivotal, serving as an irreplaceable force that drives our journey. Artificial motions shall never surpass human emotions, where the seeds of humanity persist.

1

CHALLENGING TIMES; INTELLECTUAL PLEASURE

I would like to dream of peacefully dying where I'm really dying.

~

Slavoj Žižek
Slovenian philosopher, cultural theorist and public intellectual.

WE SAT down on one Sunday evening around 5:30 in Ljubljana time, which was 8:30 in the evening here in Colombo. Year, 2023. The purpose was not to delve into deep philosophical realms but rather to listen to Slavoj Žižek's thoughts on a few prevailing social issues. It had been a longstanding dream of mine to convey his ideas to the general public, which is tired of jargon and seeks great ideas in simple language. I first started communicating with Slavoj Žižek, the intellectual superstar known for his unstoppable yet profound talks in any public gathering. I owe this opportunity to David J. Gunkel of Northern Illinois University, with whom I had my very first discussion about this eminent philosopher approximately seven years ago. This Slovenian philosopher, armed with a humorous sense, expertly deconstructs the most serious challenges and profound ideologies, and he needs no introduction.

However, meeting Slavoj was challenging as he is currently facing health issues, including panic attacks. Being aware of this made me cautious not to tire him during our conversation. Nevertheless, as the night was still young, he passionately talked, and most of the time, I found it hard to interrupt him. However, as he jokingly suggested, I might have to use "Stalinist freedom" to condense the insights from our hour-long discussion. Slavoj displayed patience and skillfully identified points where we had to pause due to technical issues.

Stopping Slavoj when he is engrossed in conversation is quite inconvenient, and as a moderator, one might even forget their role. I shared with him that after years of communicating via email, it was my first time being in a live discussion with him, just the two of us. I jokingly remarked, "Slavoj, you are the most dangerous philosopher in the West. Oh God, you don't look dangerous," especially after hearing his brief observation on Sri Lanka during a time when its economic and political crisis dominated world headlines.

To this, Slavoj responded, "The branding of me as dangerous

is a critique against my ideas. People who call me dangerous may also label me as despicable. I believe that such descriptions, whether politically dangerous, Stalinist, fascist, or merely as a joker, are used to undermine the seriousness of my work. Despite my jokes and provocations, I genuinely enjoy writing them. I'll let you in on a secret: recently, New Statesman published three of my film reviews on Indiana Jones, Barbie, and Oppenheimer. Interestingly, I hadn't seen any of these movies when I wrote the reviews. Instead, I read many reviews on them and then wrote my own. However, upon watching the films later, I realized that my initial assessments were accurate."

This is Slavoj Žižek—timeless, ever-engaging, and ensuring you won't be bored when listening to him. Instead, he invites you to dive deep into the dizzying world of intellectual discourse.

I decided to limit this conversation to eight major questions and twelve key words at the end. Stopping Slavoj from answering any question was challenging; he has a natural inclination to talk, but I believe that's the nature of this profoundly honest philosopher who attracts minds from across the globe. In Sri Lanka, some social groups embraced Slavoj's ideological perspectives, but I don't think they penetrated deeply enough among the youth and other social segments thirsty for real structural change. These groups not only indulge in political vulgarity but also shy away from much-needed ideological-based social discourse. Meanwhile, certain groups and individuals confine themselves to their comfort zones, avoiding engagement with the pressing social and economic issues in society.

During our intriguing conversation, my interlocutor expressed an initial assurance of what he humorously referred to as 'Stalinist freedom.' He playfully remarked, 'I will allow you to exercise Stalinist freedom, where I talk without hesitation, and you can sharply censor my words.' This prompted my first question, wherein I inquired what Slavoj Žižek's opening lines would be if he had the opportunity to confront Joseph Stalin during his era. To my surprise, he responded, 'I think he's not personally a bad guy, but he caused an irreversible catastrophe for the left. While so-called Stalinism is discredited as a serious idea in new socialist borders, I'm not sure if I'd have enough courage to do it, but if invited to meet him somehow, even at the risk of being liquidated instantly, I'd like to take the chance to kill him. Yes, I will kill him,' he declared.

However, what interests him the most is the opportunity to meet Vladimir Lenin at the end of his life and ask him, "Was he still aware of what a monster he was creating?" Slavoj says that while Stalin isn't stupid, he lacks a profound decree. People often expect that someone as super powerful as a dictator is possess some deep metaphysical wisdom. For instance, during the Khmer Rouge's dominance in Cambodia (Kampuchea), they claimed that Pol Pot was highly educated in Buddhism and even attained Nirvana, arguing that it explained how he could be a monstrous leader yet appear kind in person. Slavoj rejects this argument, stating, "I don't buy into this. I don't think we should look for some deep, even diabolic wisdom in brutal dictators."

This leads me to my next question, as Slavoj has not only spoken about Western philosophy but also expressed his understandings of Buddhism and how it influences both itself and society, including the West. I asked him how Buddhist monks can effectively navigate involvement in politics while addressing societal challenges and avoiding ideological pitfalls.

"It is no less different for them than for others. Having studied a bit of the history and presence of Buddhism and being aware of the danger of speaking from my European standpoint, I have examined what is gaining popularity now, not only in the East but also in the West—Buddhist economists. One in the West, I believe, is E. F. Schumacher, who wrote 'Small Is Beautiful' along those lines. I am skeptical here. It is easy to see the insights propagated by Buddhist economists, although I don't consider it a closed teaching. Some of their advice is pragmatically interesting, offering non-violent, utopian claims on how to radically change society. However, I always look at this with a critical eye. For instance, when their ideas were challenged and asked to prove their effectiveness, they often mentioned Bhutan, a country known for maintaining Gross National Happiness. Yet, in the early nineties, didn't they conduct a fairly sharp ethnic cleansing? They expelled the Lhotshampa or Nepalese minority, which is precisely contrary to Gross National Happiness. It's always a problem," he observed.

Slavoj believes that a serious problem emerged right after Buddha's death, where tendencies arose to seek accommodation with those in power. "Even in the case of Sri Lanka, feel free to correct me if I'm wrong, as I don't buy into most of the Western media narratives. There were certain ways in which the Buddhist majority could have acted differently when it came to minority issues. The irony is that true Buddhists understand this and never take things at face value. Buddhism cannot be conceived as a religion in the Western sense. We must remember that Buddha was explicitly agnostic about suffering, seeing it as a fundamental aspect of life, and his focus was on how to alleviate suffering rather than delving into great metaphysical questions," he said.

"I would say that, in my references to Zen Buddhism in Japan most of the time, which defended Japanese colonization, there is much to learn from Buddhism today to address certain issues like ecological catastrophe—not just by advocating "not to kill worms," but by taking individual responsibility to address the consequences of capitalism and its dynamics. Buddhism, in its original forms—not some kind of fanatical view on renouncing life to potentially become monks and seek Nirvana—is a wonderful pragmatic and agnostic view. From its very inception, Buddhism detected the falsity of excessive social engagements not driven by progressive causes but by expansionism and the like. Buddhism should do more in this regard. I would say that it's not just for monks; even ordinary people who follow Buddhism can contribute. You don't have to act like a perfect monk, but maintaining common decency is essential. What saddens me today is that this fundamental aspect is disappearing more and more from society," he asserted.

"Today, we witness new forms of evil that present themselves as good, but in challenging situations like war and social upheaval, the greatest danger lies in abandoning our fundamental human kindness. In such circumstances, the idea of being brutal becomes prominent. This is where Buddhism can help, as Buddhism has never endorsed this approach," Slavoj stated.

My next question was whether there is such a thing as a "just society," or if it's merely a collective myth we fool ourselves with. However, for Slavoj, the problem lies in defining what we mean by a just society. The traditional idea, originating not in the West but from Buddha, viewed justice as everyone having their designated place, such as workers being good workers, mothers being good mothers, and so on. But both in Buddhism and later in Christianity, in their original forms, there emerged a more radical egalitarian space advocating the idea of equality, where everyone has a social space. The most crucial aspect is expanding this egalitarian space without resorting to violence, as any attempt at violence only reinforces brutal hierarchies. Therefore, the first step towards a just society is to clarify the meaning of justice by understanding what justice truly is, he argued.

In our increasingly AI-shaped world, the question arises: should we fear the rise of "Artificial Idiocy"? Will machines not only surpass humans in intelligence but also in their ability to make absurd mistakes? According to Slavoj, these machines are indeed making mistakes, but what matters is how we define "Absurd Mistakes." As he tried to develop in his book "Hegel in

A Wired Brain," human intelligence is not simply about quick calculations and solving certain complex issues; it excels when it comes to making productive mistakes that lead to something new and higher. For instance, French cuisine's most celebrated dishes often originated from something going wrong, like French cheese that started to smell. Instead of discarding it, they embraced the new form. The same happened with wines. This capacity to use mistakes productively and elevate from them is something he doubts AI can achieve. Machines can make mistakes, but they lack the ability to utilize those mistakes to create something better. He takes a more vulgar example, like seduction, where he believes machines can't seduce as humans do, not because of intelligence, but because of the ability to make interesting mistakes. Progress, Slavoj says, occurs only through the productive use of mistakes.

Based on perhaps my superficial phobia of AI, my next question revolved around the possibility of advanced AI engaging in philosophical debates like Slavoj Žižek, while robotic comedians mock human foibles, and AI-driven revolutionary movements fight for workers' rights and robot liberation. Slavoj dismisses this possibility, explaining that when humans make decisions, they always do so through subjective engagement. He cites his favorite Christian theologian Søren Kierkegaard, who wrote that claiming to be Christian, Buddhist, Jew, or anything else because you compare different religions and find Christian arguments the best is sinful. True understanding of religious arguments can only occur when you believe in something expediently. Similarly, when it comes to love, you cannot say you compare different individuals and selected the best. Love doesn't work that way; it's based on finding adorable qualities that others might not even recognize. He believes that, at least for now, as nobody knows what the future holds, machines are incapable of engaging in proper subjective engagement where they discover reasons rather than merely comparing them because they are searching for the right reason.

In this sense, I don't believe machines can fight for workers' rights and similar causes. Engaging in workers' rights requires an existential understanding of suffering, such as exploitation and manipulation, which cannot be reduced to objective scientific insights. I admit I may not be overly optimistic, but that's my view," he asserted.

Many discussions revolve around the loss of privacy due to the latest surveillance technology and social media. I asked Slavoj about the danger of governments and corporations gathering vast amounts of personal data, leading us to sacrifice privacy for convenience. He responded, "I'm unlike many others who fear losing privacy. I don't mind if some machines know my personal details, but what worries me most is the privatization of our data. We don't know what they know or what they do with that data. Our focus should not be solely on defending privacy, as more and more machines will gather data and analyze our needs, such as health. What concerns me is the privatization of our data and shrinking public space."

As virtual reality becomes more prevalent in our lives, I asked Slavoj about the safeguards needed to prevent the distortion of reality and preserve authentic human experiences. He explained, "What we experience as social reality is already, in some sense, virtual. I'm not denying the existence of reality, but what we perceive as reality is already mediated through a virtual symbolic system. Take the recent movie Oppenheimer, for example. The horror of a nuclear explosion is something that exceeds our notion of everyday reality. The distortion in virtual media doesn't target some pure, innocent reality; it affects the authentic virtual reality of the system in which we live. Authenticity, for me, is not merely looking into oneself; it involves identifying with a certain heroic engagement. The problem with digital media is that they are becoming less and less virtual. Instead of offering metaphors, alluded meanings, and ambiguity, they strive for a perfect copy of reality itself.

Take video games as an example—they immerse you in another reality, but in doing so, they lose this authentic virtual quality."

---

12 WORDS ŽIŽEK UNFILTERED

MARRIAGE	I almost like more and more marriage as, at least in developing parts of the world, marriage is no longer about distorting economic funds but more about giving a slap to societal vulgarity, which is very beautiful.
EMANCIPATION	Like justice the problem lies in the interpretation; if it's understood as mere legal equality, as Marx has convincingly shown, it can result in a new form of oppression, and I believe true emancipation requires a continuous struggle to redefine it due to the historical atrocities committed in its name, such as John Locke's justification for the annihilation of native Indians.
CAPITALISM	I cannot agree with much of what people in the Global South say, but we have to go through it.
IDEOLOGICAL FANTASY	One must remember that fantasy is not the opposite of reality, as fantasies already decide how we perceive reality.
VLADIMIR PUTIN	Almost the same view I have had on Joseph Stalin; I think he is a mega catastrophe for Russia. If his intentions win, we are entering a neo-feudalism.
GLOBAL SOUTH	In principle, I agree that the Global South is a victim of colonialism and neo-colonization, but it has its own issues far greater than the consequences of colonial masters, and they will not be solved simply by getting rid of neo-colonialism.
LOVE	I like love in its exclusive violent aspect, where love is a catastrophe—you may lose everything, but you still love it.
AI IN HOLLYWOOD	The problem is not just the fear of losing jobs for writers and actresses, but also what kind of machine Hollywood will allow and what kind of stories it will demand.

FUTURE COMMUNISM	It is something that can only come about through a radical change in society, and our society has no future, but it needs a new beginning.
WEST WITHOUT WHISTLEBLOWERS	The worst of all possible worlds.
DEATH	Although we are mortal beings, I like to speculate in vampire movies called 'undeathness' or living death, which captures our struggle for emancipation, similar to what we see in terminators.
LAST DREAM	I would like to dream of peacefully dying where I'm really dying.

As we near the conclusion of this intriguing conversation, I asked Slavoj about escaping consumerist culture and finding authentic freedom, as discussed in his critiques of capitalism. He replied, "I'm more pessimistic about this. We live in a global capitalist society where we appear to be increasingly free. On one hand, we are treated as free, but at the same time, we are part of a social world that is obscured and non-transparent. So, we need to clarify what we mean by freedom. I don't believe we should oppose freedom, discipline, and social order. Abstractly, freedom might mean doing whatever we want, but I wouldn't want to live in such a society because it would be a horrible world if we couldn't trust each other to respect basic rules of decency. True freedom requires explicit and implicit rules to be in operation."

Regarding consumerism, he added, "When you talk about the upper middle-class, the problem might be consumerism, but for a poor person, the issue is getting new clothes and adequate food. We shouldn't criticize poor people for consumerism when they finally get a bit of money to buy something they need. Let them have a bit of pleasure. For me, the crucial aspect, in a Hegelian sense, is that freedom has to be concrete. Freedom means being free within a certain space, which is why we should strive for socialist democracy as leftists. We must understand that freedom has material conditions. I'm not advocating for a totalitarian state regulating every aspect of life. I like the form of freedom, but to achieve it, a full concrete network of state regulations, unwritten rules, and customs must be well established. Unfortunately, this is something people tend to forget today.

During the final part of our conversation, we delved into several issues, including multiculturalism, the idea of a multi-polar world, the hypocritical behavior of Western hegemony, and the brutal sexual exploitation faced by some Muslim women who are forced to cover their faces to protect their privacy, yet suffer abuse within their homes, rendering their privacy futile. Slavoj expressed his belief in the universality as a driving force to promote respect for each culture. "There must be freedom for me to come over there when I have a problem, and you must have the freedom to come over here when you have a problem in the place where you live. That's how the idea of this multi-polar world or multiculturalism is possible," he emphasized. "No the way by romanticizing and pleasing each other's oppressions in the country they control."

2

WISDOM IN
POLITICAL INSIGHTS

I believe that stepping down from the position of prime
minister was a significant mistake.

~

Mahathir Bin Mohamad
Malaysian Politician, Author, and Physician who served as
Prime Minister of Malaysia

BEFORE we dive into the world of politics, I was eager to learn how he managed his style and which fundamentals he followed to pursue the goal of the common good. I had the privilege of sitting down with none other than Mahathir Mohamad, the luminary force behind Malaysia's ascendancy. Yet, before he became an icon in the political arena, Mahathir Mohamad was a physician, a graduate of the esteemed King Edward VII College of Medicine in Singapore. I sought his wisdom on the enduring principles that guide a life and a profession.

As he leaned forward, his eyes reflecting the wisdom of a life well-lived, he shared, 'If I may speak of my calling as a medical doctor, there is one cardinal principle that reigns supreme – the patient's well-being. It's not about profiting from others' misfortunes but about tirelessly working towards healing. In my practice, I encountered countless individuals grappling with life's myriad challenges.'

Dr. Mahathir bin Mohamad, a towering figure in Asian politics, helmed the office of Prime Minister for an astounding 24 years, from 1981 to 2003 and later from 2018 to 2020. He revealed a philosophy that has been his compass throughout this remarkable journey.

'I lead a life of moderation, avoiding the extremes. For instance, when I eat, I do so in moderation, sufficient for sustenance. My mother's wisdom echoes in my ears – when food becomes overly delightful, it's time to stop. Moderation, in all aspects of life, is key. Never veer to the extremes,' he advised with a serene smile.

In explaining his longevity, he shared, 'I abstain from smoking and drinking, and I refrain from overindulgence in food. I consume just what is necessary for my vitality.'

Turning to the subject of knowledge, he harked back to his foundational beliefs. 'Knowledge has eternally held sway. The ancient Egyptians didn't erect pyramids through divine incantations, nor did the waters flow in the irrigation canals of the Indus Civilization by the ignorance of their laws. Knowledge has perpetually been the font of power and prosperity.'

Mahathir stands as one of the senior-most active politicians in Asia, if not the world, having borne witness to the ascents and declines of countless leaders. When I inquired about those whom he admired and those who presented challenges, he narrated with a gleam of respect in his eyes.

'There are leaders I greatly admire, striving to emulate their approach to problem-solving. Take Nelson Mandela, who endured over 27 years in captivity yet emerged without a trace of bitterness, working hand in hand with his former captors to rebuild South Africa. He exemplified selflessness, prioritizing society over self. Leaders of this caliber endure suffering for the greater good of humanity.'

As for the more trying encounters he encountered during his tenure, *he gracefully refrained from singling them out, understanding the potential consequences it could have on individuals and their families.*

To encapsulate our conversation, I posed a question that goes to the core of leadership: 'What, in your view, are the defining qualities of a true statesperson? How does one distinguish a genuine leader from someone who exploits racial or religious elements for power?'

With a measured tone, he responded, 'A true statesperson is one who places the world and society above personal interests. Even when faced with personal hurt, they remain committed to what is right and beneficial for the common citizen.'

Next, our conversation delved into the profound impact of nationalism on the process of nation-building. I sought

Mahathir's insights on the pivotal role of nationalism and how he harnessed this concept during his tenure as Malaysia's leader, even in the face of contentious allegations regarding anti-Semitic rhetoric, favoritism towards the ethnic Malay majority, and the treatment of political opponents.

In response, he articulated, 'First and foremost, one must cultivate a deep love for their country. It's the place where you were born, raised, and achieved your aspirations; essentially, it's where your roots lie. This genuine love for one's nation fosters a sincere desire to contribute to its development. When you hold authentic affection for your country, the thought of causing harm or tarnishing its reputation becomes inconceivable.'

He continued, 'When individuals feel that their nation is capable of self-sustenance, it instills a sense of pride and responsibility. This sentiment, at its core, embodies the essence of true nationalism. Once a common goal is attained, there arises no inclination to harm the country.'

Shifting gears, I delved into the remarkable economic transformation Malaysia underwent during his leadership. In 1981, when he assumed office, Malaysia's GDP stood at approximately 25 billion USD. Under his visionary stewardship, the nation's GDP burgeoned to a staggering 110.2 billion USD. Many attribute this success to his leadership, despite its association with contentious policies. I inquired about the secrets behind this economic triumph.

His response carried the weight of experience, 'To foster a nation's growth, stability and peace are imperative. A nation beset by instability and racial tensions cannot thrive. In Malaysia, a diverse and multicultural country, my foremost task was to unite people from various ethnic and religious backgrounds to work together, thereby establishing social stability and peace. Once this foundation is laid, the path is paved for economic growth, attracting new investments, and enabling individuals from diverse fields to flourish professionally.'

Turning to his interactions with Sri Lanka, a country he had visited multiple times, I couldn't help but pose a question about the nation's divergent trajectory compared to Malaysia and Singapore. In the face of this, he offered his perspective with characteristic composure.

'You've made several visits to Sri Lanka, with your last visit in 2014, during which you launched various development projects. At one point, you and your political rival, the late Lee Kuan Yew, emphasized the importance of learning from Sri Lanka's successes. However, today, Sri Lanka's path diverges significantly from that of Malaysia and Singapore. What, in your opinion, went wrong in Sri Lanka?' I inquired.

With sagacity, he observed, 'A country's progress is greatly contingent on its leadership. If the leader is inept, unfocused on authentic national development, or lacks an understanding of what development model suits their nation, regression is inevitable. History is replete with examples of countries that once shone brightly but have since faded.'

He continued, 'Some nations falter when leaders prioritize personal gain and well-being over the welfare of the nation. Consequently, regression becomes the destiny. The history of every country exhibits cycles of ups and downs, and change is an intrinsic part of a nation's journey.'

Mahathir's spirited political debates with the late Lee Kuan Yew of Singapore remain indelibly etched in the annals of history, captivating audiences worldwide. In a book titled 'Conversations with Mahathir Mohamad,' he offered a glimpse into the dynamic, remarking, 'The fact remains that he is a mayor of Singapore. This is something he doesn't like. He wants to be big, you see, and he feels that we took away his opportunity to lead a real country.' Conversely, Lee Kuan Yew referred to Mahathir as 'a thoroughly destructive force. He is a very smart man, but his mentality is still stuck in the 1970s.' I probed him to reflect on those years of fervent political rivalry and the intricacies of their relationship.

With a gentle smile, he journeyed back in time, recounting, 'When Singapore merged with Malaysia, it was a nation struggling to find its footing. Emerging from British rule, it had encountered its share of challenges during that period. Lee Kuan Yew saw this merger as his chance to become the Prime Minister of Malaysia. In Malaysia, he believed he could hold a substantial role, akin to a real Prime Minister, whereas in Singapore, he would be more like a mayor. However, he soon discovered that Malaysia was not as welcoming as he had hoped. Ultimately, Malaysia expelled Singapore due to the disruptive political climate he had introduced. The then Prime Minister, Tunku Abdul Rahman, decided that Singapore should no longer be part of Malaysia. Singapore, of course, thrived after its expulsion, but at that moment, Lee Kuan Yew believed he had lost a significant opportunity to become a Prime Minister, which is why he shed tears.'

Responding to Lee Kuan Yew's characterization of him, he remarked, 'Well, everyone is entitled to their perspective. He viewed me as orthodox, and perhaps he wasn't entirely wrong. I was deeply concerned about racial relations in Malaysia. We have three major ethnic groups, but their achievements were not on par. The Chinese community had made significant strides and seized opportunities post-independence, while the Malays struggled in business, despite being afforded similar opportunities. This disparity was a persistent obstacle to our nation's development. My aim was to eliminate these disparities and drive the country toward true development. To some, my methods might have seemed orthodox, but my focus was squarely on bridging the ethnic divides.'

Shifting our conversation, I inquired about reports suggesting that during his tenure as Prime Minister of Malaysia, he had made efforts to secure ASEAN membership for Sri Lanka but faced opposition from certain political quarters in other countries. I asked him to confirm the accuracy of these reports.

He responded thoughtfully, 'Indeed, ASEAN is a remarkable success story in the realm of regional cooperation, notably for its ability to reject war in the region for over six decades. While many other nations expressed interest in joining ASEAN, certain factors, such as geographical location, posed obstacles to their inclusion. The organization's concern was that if it expanded too rapidly, it might become unwieldy.'

He continued, 'I believed Sri Lanka was a suitable candidate for ASEAN membership, transcending geographical differences. However, other member nations were hesitant to extend the invitation.'

Next, I aimed to glean his perspective on a crucial aspect of leadership – the development of secondary leadership. Often, exceptional leaders, when they depart, leave behind a void that can lead to political polarization and division. I queried how he, drawing from his decades of political experience and wisdom, fostered secondary leadership in Malaysia and navigated the challenges along the way.

He began by emphasizing the responsibility that comes with power, saying, 'When you assume the role of Prime Minister, you wield immense power, and that power can be either a tool for personal gain or an instrument for national progress. I was acutely aware that if I used that power for personal purposes, I would tarnish my legacy and leave a stain on the nation's history. Instead, I chose to focus on the nation's development. For me, the enduring satisfaction came from witnessing the country's growth. That was the only reward I sought, and it was the reward I received from the world through recognition of Malaysia's development.'

He continued, 'During my first term as Prime Minister, which lasted for over twenty years, I realized that it was a lengthy tenure, and I was already in my seventies. I firmly believed that the key to our nation's progress lay in nurturing a new generation of leaders. I advocated for the notion that developing the nation was a prerequisite for individual growth. I encouraged my successors to follow the same path, with the aim of propelling Malaysia to developed nation status. However, once I stepped down from office, subsequent leaders pursued different agendas. They wrongly believed that during my tenure, I had misappropriated government funds, despite the facts pointing to the contrary. Consequently, they began to wield their power for personal interests, derailing the path we had charted since the early '80s. This regression halted Malaysia's growth.'

He went on to recount, 'This prompted me to re-enter politics. Subsequently, I once again assumed the role of Prime Minister. However, the political landscape had transformed. Certain political parties resorted to exploiting religious and ethnic divisions to disrupt the newly formed government, triggering a series of political crises and eroding political stability. In the past sixty years, we had experienced only four changes in government. However, after my departure in 2020, four different governments came to power, further exacerbating political and social instability.'

Curious about external influences, I inquired if external parties played a role in perpetuating this instability. Dr. Mahathir acknowledged the possibility of some external elements but characterized the situation as a complex political crisis that would require time and effort to resolve.

Finally, I posed a poignant question: What he considered to be his biggest mistake during his tenure as the longest-serving ruler in modern Malaysian history. He contemplated this deeply and replied, 'I believe that stepping down from the position of Prime Minister was a significant mistake. However, had I not done so, people would not have had the opportunity to see what kind of government they would get in my absence. It's often during challenging times that we truly appreciate the value of a nation's well-being. We must undergo difficult periods to realize that the prosperity of a country is not a permanent state.

As our captivating conversation neared its conclusion, I sought Dr. Mahathir's wisdom on the pressing issues that confront our world today. In this era of multiple crises – from global health emergencies to supply chain disruptions, debates surrounding multi-polarism versus Western hegemony, the rise of the Global South, and China's aspirations to superpower status – I asked him to convey a message to the global community, one that promotes equity and dignity for all of humanity.

With a deep historical perspective, he reflected, 'In the past, when conflicts arose among small principalities, strong leaders would unite these territories into larger nations, steering them towards development. That was the historical narrative. However, our world has changed significantly. Today, due to the ease of communication, we are not just neighbors with our immediate neighboring countries but with the entire world. This closeness brings with it shared challenges that demand a collective approach. In essence, we require a form of global governance.'"

He continued, 'We have seen attempts at this before, such as the League of Nations, which ultimately faltered. Then came the era of the United Nations, which, unfortunately, is also facing challenges. The United Nations, with its five veto-wielding powers, can sometimes be stymied by the interests of a few. Therefore, it is imperative for the world to forge a unified movement to tackle common global issues, including pandemics, the consequences of climate change, the growing global population, and more. Just as small principalities once came together to form nation-states, now nation-states must unite to create a global governance structure capable of addressing these shared problems.'

As a parting thought, Dr. Mahathir turned his attention to the ongoing conflict in Ukraine. He observed, 'Europeans still seem to contemplate resolving international conflicts through wars. They had allied with the Russians during World War II to combat Germany, and together they defeated Germany. However, immediately after victory, they designated Russia as a new enemy, leading to the establishment of NATO, focused squarely on Russia. In response, Russia formed the Warsaw Pact, sparking a prolonged Cold War, which was a considerable waste of resources and time. When Russia eventually decided to dissolve the Warsaw Pact, NATO took a different path. Instead of dismantling itself, it bolstered its capabilities and invited former Warsaw Pact members to join, all directed against Russia. This inevitably fueled a series of conflicts, with the Ukraine conflict being a part of this larger narrative.'"

He concluded with a resounding call for change, stating, 'While NATO nations provide support to the war in Ukraine, it is the Ukrainian people who are fighting and suffering. Allowing Ukrainians to endure this conflict, with lives lost and their nation in ruins, is untenable. The mindset of resolving disputes through warfare must come to an end.'

3

COLONIAL LEGACIES AND POST-COLONIAL REALITIES

The journey out of the neo-colonial structures is not easy.

~

Vijay Prashad
Indian historian, author, journalist, political commentator, and Marxist intellectual.

THE KEY lessons from the history of anti-colonial struggles emphasize the importance of hard work, patience, and sacrifice in building mass movements for liberation, self-determination, and social justice. These lessons serve as inspiration and guidance for contemporary movements striving to achieve similar goals in our present times.

In this insightful discussion, Vijay Prashad, a prominent Indian historian and commentator, shared his valuable insights on various subjects, including the role of the Indian diaspora in shaping global perspectives on Indian politics and culture, his motivation to study the intersections of imperialism, capitalism, and globalization, and the enduring effects of colonialism on India and other colonized nations. Through his profound knowledge and expertise, Prashad provided thought-provoking perspectives that shed light on significant historical and contemporary issues.

As the Director of the Tricontinental: Institute for Social Research, Prashad continues to shape critical discourse and provoke thoughtful analysis. Prashad has authored numerous influential publications, which serve as intellectual milestones in understanding historical and contemporary issues. With a profound understanding of global politics, Prashad's works unravel the intricate intersections between power, culture, and resistance, offering invaluable insights into the complexities of our world.

Excerpts of the interview;

Question [Q]: As an Indian historian and commentator, how do you see the role of the Indian diaspora in shaping global perspectives on Indian politics and culture?

Answer [A]: The Indian diaspora is varied, oscillating between people who have almost no politics to people who are adherents of the far-right. There was a time when the Indian diaspora was the home of the Left. The first left-wing Indian political party was established in California in 1913. It was the Ghadar Party. Many of those who were attracted to it later went to the USSR to learn how to become Communists, and then went on to join the Communist movement in India. The Communist Party of India was founded in Tashkent (USSR) in 1920, mostly by emigré Indians, a different kind of diaspora. But, after independence, the nature of migration changed, as sections of the Indian middle-class left the country for economic reasons and their political life mirrored the journey of the Indian middle-class within the country. The middle-class Indian diaspora today is the exact complement of the Indian middle-class inside India.

Q: What motivated you to study and write about the intersection of imperialism, capitalism, and globalization, particularly in relation to the Global South?

A: I was born and brought up in Kolkata, India, which is a city of great marvels but also a city of immense inequality. To people like me, born into education and means, the striking aspect of our lives was the gap between what we experienced and the absolute devastation of poverty that defined the lives of people around us. That social inequality hit me hard and continues to strike me. It is what forced me to learn about why inequality is reproduced, to seek answers from the facts, and therefore to discover that the source of such inequality was the ugly profit-driven system of capitalism that had absorbed wretched hierarchies that predate capitalism, such as the caste system. Why was India not able to transcend the caste hierarchies and the ugliness of capitalism? It was not just because of the greed of the Indian bourgeoise and the landlords, but also due to the immense power of the neo-colonial structure maintained by the former colonial powers. You can't understand the poverty on the streets of Colombo, for instance, without having a full understanding of the imperialist system.

Q: In your work, you often highlight the impact of imperialism on the countries and regions it has affected. How would you describe the lasting effects of imperialism on India and other colonized nations?

A: Firstly, it is important to note that British imperialism – which ruled India for centuries – stole tens of trillions of pounds from the Indian people. Several economists have tried to calculate this enormous 'drain of wealth'. Profits made in India and wealth built in India were not reinvested in the country but taken and invested in the United Kingdom. This led to a cascade of underinvestment in India, and therefore the impoverishment of the country. Second, as a consequence of this underinvestment – the lack of use of capital formed in India – was that there was reduced employment opportunities for the people, including lack of investment in agriculture that led to the catastrophic famines of the Victorian Era. Third, the British imperial state in India failed to invest in social development – namely in health and education – which grievously impacted the living conditions of people. When the British were booted out of India, the literacy rate was a mere 13% (in the UK, during the same period, the literacy rate was about 98%). These three impacts – theft of capital to the UK, the underinvestment in Indian agriculture, and the lack of social investment – have had long-term, catastrophic impacts on India.

Q: Some critics argue that anti-imperialist movements and ideologies often romanticize and idealize certain regimes or leaders, even when they may have engaged in oppressive practices. How do you respond to these critiques, and how can anti-imperialist movements avoid falling into this trap?

A: The journey out of the neo-colonial structures is not easy. People in very poor countries, with backward state institutions, struggle to establish their sovereignty over their territory and to create dignity for their people. They face attacks ceaselessly, which often leads beleaguered states to turn inward. The problems within the path of anti-colonial projects are nothing compared to the problems that structure those failures, namely the neo-colonial system. It is convenient for the old colonial powers to point fingers at the problems inside the post-colonial states, but harder for them to accept their own role in creating the enabling conditions for state failure and oppressive practices.

Q: What are some key challenges faced by post-colonial countries in achieving economic and political sovereignty, and how can they address these challenges effectively?

A: The most important challenges are two: first, the obduracy of the old colonial powers who refuse to allow for sovereignty and thereby use any means (including invasions and coups) to hold onto power (even if they allow for flag independence), and second, the theft of wealth by the colonial powers that leaves the new states in a dependent relation to their former colonial rulers, but this time not through political power but through economic interconnections. If a post-colonial state tries to establish its sovereignty over its own territory and raw materials (such as Chile in the early 1970s), it faces economic sabotage and then a coup (1973). This story repeats itself over and over again.

Q: Your work often critiques Western interventionism and imperialism. However, some argue that there are instances where international intervention can be justified, such as in cases of genocide or human rights abuses. How do you navigate this complex ethical terrain?

A: Obviously, there must be room for external intervention in times of genuine genocide. That principle is not established by the United Nations. However, that principle is also misused by the West to fulfill its own aims. For instance, it used the term genocide to justify the destruction of Libya in 2011 (after the bombardment ended, Amnesty International showed that there was nothing like genocide happening in Libya). Furthermore, Western interventions – such as in Iraq – have led to massive destruction (including loss of life and human rights abuses). We need to be very careful when we hear talk of genocide, since the term has been used instrumentally by Western powers to justify their own military interventions for their own narrow imperialist ends.

Q: The concept of "third worldism" has been central to your analysis. Could you explain this concept and its relevance in today's global context?

A: Actually, I do not use this term, since the term itself is not precise enough. I use the term 'Third World Project' to specify the social dynamic set in place at the tail end of the colonial era, when colonized states got together to drive a combined agenda against the neo-colonial system. These states met in Bandung, Indonesia in 1955, and then later established the Non-Aligned Movement in 1961. This Third World Project was destroyed in the 1980s during the Third World debt crisis, when they lost their political strength due to the devastation of their economies and the use by the West of the International Monetary Fund to damage the integrity of the new states. Today, we have a different context, different possibilities. That is our history.

Q: Marxist ideologies have been widely criticized for their historical association with authoritarian regimes. How do you address these criticisms, and what do you believe is the role of Marxism in building a just and inclusive society?

A: The term 'authoritarian regime' is an ideological term. Its most scientific basis was provided by Hannah Arendt in her The Origins of Totalitarianism (1951), which made the case that fascism and communism are much the same thing. The association between fascism and communism is not only analytically lazy but it performed a task for the Western imperialist states that wanted to defame communism despite the historical role played by the USSR in the destruction of Nazism. So, what do we mean by authoritarian regimes? We do not add in their list the totalitarian regimes set in place by Western imperialism after the coups in Iran (1953) and Guatemala (1954), nor the money-driven democracies in the West that have corrupted democracy and driven people into either total social passivity or neo-fascist rage. Marxists stand against these kinds of totalitarianisms.

Q: Climate change is an urgent issue facing the world today. What are your thoughts on the responsibility of wealthy nations in addressing climate justice and supporting the Global South in tackling environmental challenges?

A: My thoughts are not as significant as the treaty obligations of the Western powers, who signed the 1992 Rio framework of 'common but differentiated responsibilities', which means that they recognize the common problems of environmental destruction and climate change but see that there are differentiated responsibilities based on the historical abuse of the planet by the imperialist powers. This is a treaty obligation. And yet, the West has not lived up to their own obligation. They should be taken to the International Criminal Court for this malfeasance.

Q: Your book "The Darker Nations" focuses on the rise of the Non-Aligned Movement and the Bandung Conference. How do you view the relevance and legacy of these movements in the present-day geopolitical landscape?

A: Today, the context of that period when the Third World Project shone is very different. Certain states in the developing world – China, India, Brazil, Mexico, Indonesia, South Africa – have taken on an important role in global leadership. The establishment of the BRICS (2009) and the emergence of the New Non-Alignment has opened up new possibilities. This opening is built on the legacy of the past, but it does not repeat them. These large states no longer want to accept the claim by the West that their parochial interests are universal. These states want to put forward their own national interests. We have to closely study this New Non-Alignment.

Q: Identity politics has become a contentious topic in recent years. What is your perspective on the role of identity-based movements in social and political struggles, and how can they contribute to broader movements for justice and equality?

A: The term identity politics is very general. Of course, there are historical social hierarchies – such as the caste system and patriarchy – that have to be frontally challenged and defeated. These will take place by broad based struggles against caste and patriarchy. An idea has come to the fore that only the victims of these systems can fight in this struggle. This narrows the fight and makes it weaker. We need to assemble broad based struggles of all people to fight to liberate humanity from wretchedness.

Q: How do you view the relationship between Marxism and anti-imperialism? Do you think Marxism provides an effective framework for addressing the unique challenges faced by post-colonial societies?

A: Marxism is one of the only frameworks that properly addresses the crisis-ridden system of capitalism that produces imperialist tendencies amongst its most powerful countries. No other theory of the world properly explains the cycle of crises and the punctuality of wars. If another theory comes along, let me know.

Q: However, some argue that globalization and capitalism, despite their flaws, have brought significant economic development and lifted millions out of poverty. How do you respond to this argument, and what alternative economic models do you propose?

A: If you look at the UN data, you will find that the country that has lifted the most number of people out of poverty is China. And the Chinese people have not eradicated absolute poverty through globalization and capitalism. They have done so, as our Tricontinental study shows, by the central work of the Communist Party of China and the state apparatus, which in a very studious and clear way went after certain social problems that had to be overcome for poverty to be eradicated. Countries that have weakened state structures – a necessary byproduct of extreme neoliberalism – have seen their poverty rates rise.

Q: Your analysis often focuses on the negative impacts of imperialism and capitalism. However, can you acknowledge any positive aspects or unintended consequences that may have emerged from these systems?

A: Can't see any.

Q: In your view, what are some key lessons that can be drawn from the history of anti-colonial struggles, and how can they inform and inspire contemporary movements striving for liberation, self-determination, and social justice?

A: The most important lesson is from the hard work of the people who built these movements, their patience in working to establish the mass character of their movements, and the sacrifices they underwent to establish their movements and our freedom. Hard work, patience, and sacrifice: three things that we have to learn for our own times.

Q: In conclusion, as artificial intelligence continues to advance, there are concerns about its potential impact on the global workforce. How do you envision the future of work in a world increasingly driven by AI, and what steps can be taken to mitigate any negative effects on employment?

A: Capitalism necessary applies the latest in science to enhance the productive forces, whose advancement lifts the productivity rate but then eventually leads to crisis upon crisis as the rate of profit falls. This is a cycle of increased productivity and then heightened crisis that has been ongoing since the late 19th century. AI is just the latest in a new technological breakthrough. The only way to mitigate the negative impact of unemployment is to socialize the gains from productivity, which is another way of saying to transcend capitalism and go to socialism.

4

FADING DEMOCRACY IN SRI LANKA

Without a correct foreign policy, you cannot sustain a
successful diplomacy.

~

Dayan Jayatilleka
Sri Lankan academic, diplomat, writer and politician

DAYAN Jayatilleka is a renowned political scientist in Sri Lanka who has served as a diplomat in the country and the adviser to the Presidents. He is considered to be a foremost authority on the political situation in Sri Lanka, and has played a pivotal role in shaping the country's political landscape through his expertise and advice. With a deep understanding of the complex and often deeply polarized political environment in Sri Lanka, Dr. Jayatilleka provides valuable insights into the current state of the country and its future prospects.

I sat down with Dr. Jayatilleka for an in-depth interview to gain a clearer picture of the political situation in the country. During the interview, Dr. Jayatilleka provides a detailed analysis of the current political landscape in Sri Lanka, including the major players and the various political forces that are shaping the country's future. He also discusses the challenges and opportunities facing Sri Lanka as it navigates a difficult and often contentious political environment. With his extensive knowledge and experience, Dr. Jayatilleka provides a nuanced and insightful perspective on the complex and deeply polarized political situation in the country.

Excerpts of the interview;

Question [Q]: Dayan; Thank you for joining us after a long time. What fascinates us is that you never stop writing. You continued to write under any circumstances. Tell us, why should one write?

Answer [A]: I write to illuminate and to intervene; to shed light on a subject or a situation and to change it for the better or to prevent it from getting worse. If one has knowledge about a subject it should be shared. This is especially so if the subject is in the public interest but even if not there could be even a small group interested in it which could benefit. Writing is a form of education. I am a political scientist so I write about politics as an act of education as well as intervention.

In my case there is another, more personal reason for writing. The very first memory I have is of my father sitting at a typewriter, typing. I was in my playpen! My father's last column appeared on the same day as his obituary. In that sense he is something of a role model for me.

Q: But, we can see that there are many TV shows, and newspaper columns with too much politics but lack science. What is your take as an influential political scientist?

A: Well, I did my best to apply political science and scientific political analysis in the public discourse when I had a regular TV show in Sinhala and in English on a well-known TV station, but it was interrupted during my term in Moscow as ambassador and I was not given back the show on my return from Moscow in January 2020. As for the Sinhala language newspapers I used to be interviewed by them frequently, but that too has dropped off. I am happy to have my regular column, every Thursday, in the Daily FT.

Q: Journalism is your home subject. Give us a gist of the reasons behind the decline in quality, credibility and authenticity of journalism in Sri Lanka.

A: Well, journalism is my home subject in that I was born into and raised by a journalist father, Mervyn de Silva, in whose name the pinnacle award of the annual journalism awards is named: the Mervyn de Silva Award for Excellence in Journalism. That award was not instituted by me or my father's family but by the profession itself—the Editors' Guild (of which he was founder-Editor) and the Publishers' Society. However, my mother was a teacher. So I suppose I tend to combine the two: while I am by no means a professional journalist unlike my father who rose to the top of his profession, I am a political analyst, critic, commentator and columnist who tries to educate, teach, through the medium.

I'm not sure I see a 'decline', but I see a definite change, and that's natural. It is a different generation and different times.

Q: As a person with deep roots and strong ties to this subject (journalism), do you have any recommendations you would like to give the country's media outlets?

A: Well, I can only tell them what I saw of the best journalists of an earlier time. I was privileged to meet and interact with my father's seniors too: Tarzie Vittachi and Denzil Pieris. What I know is that my father's generation of journalists read widely and thought deeply. They read books and most importantly, the best of world journalism in the English-language. The quality of their discussions and presentations, including their conversations, was very high. They were always aware of the highest international standards in their profession, and of aspiring to and maintaining them. They had a broad education in the humanities which gave them a truly international outlook. While they were thoroughly westernized, they were also deeply committed to the emancipatory project of the Third World, the global South.

Q: This year is a very interesting year not only for us, Sri Lanka but for many countries. Like us, our longstanding ally and friend Burma/Myanmar also completed 75 years as an independent nation. On the other side, Israel is also going to compete for 75 years of its establishment. Simultaneously, Palestine is commemorating 75 years of losing its statehood. More importantly, the document known as the "global constitution" UDHR is completing 75 years by December this year. Do you see any similarities between these events and do you believe there is a lot to learn from each other but yet to learn?

A: Yes, in the sense that all these anniversaries mark the post-World War II period where Nazism had been defeated; humanity had experienced the worst horrors in history at the hands of fascism; the Cold War had just commenced; Socialism had expanded offering humanity an alternative to capitalism; colonialism was breaking down and on the retreat. It was a very progressive time in the consciousness of the world.

Q: Do you agree if I say that inability to learn from history is rooted in behaviour of Sri Lankans? How can we change this?

A: It is not the inability to learn from history but the inability to teach history and point out the correct lessons. It is inability to analyze history. That is why there is an inability to learn from history.

Q: Well, let us talk about your area of expertise; recently Sri Lanka faced the UPR. More than three hours long live streaming video demonstrated the positive and negative sides of submissions and responses by the government. While watching this, I was recalling when you were in Geneva during one of the most difficult times, representing the country and telling the world what exactly happening on the ground. That was a real battle, isn't it? What is the difference between then and now?

A: Then, 14 years ago, we succeeded in persuading the overwhelming majority of the UN Human Rights Council, through reasoned argumentation, of our case. We had a stronger, more credible narrative than our critics did. As a consequence, we were able to construct a very broad coalition of member-states to support us. However, a mere six weeks after we won that vote, getting more support than even the USA has managed to get in its resolutions critical of Sri Lanka at the UNHRC, the Rajapaksa regime removed our successful team and changed our discourse, stance and strategy. Our victory held for three years and then Sri Lanka began to lose serially because our vote base, including in the global south, had been eroded. We lost in 2012, 2013, 2014 under the Rajapaksas—though I was serving as Ambassador to France and they could have sent me back to Geneva after I had completed my assignment by January 2013.

Then we had the Yahapalanaya government with the UNP – Ranil and Mangala –handling foreign policy and they abjectly surrendered in Geneva, co-sponsoring a resolution which commended and was based upon UN Human Rights High Commissioner Zeid al Hussain's Report which accused Sri Lanka of 'system-wide' i.e., not merely individual or aberrant, war crimes and crimes against humanity! Ranil and Mangala agreed to courts sitting in Sri Lanka with foreign judges, foreign prosecutors and foreign counsel!

Finally the Rajapaksas returned and we resumed our losing streak, getting dwindling support every time.

Now the two sides which ruined us in Geneva—the Rajapaksas and Ranil—are together, and the result is still a disaster.

What is radically different between Geneva 2009 and Geneva 2012-2023, is that in May 2009, the immediate aftermath of a long and bloody war and with massive demonstrations by the Tamil Diaspora in Europe including Geneva, outcries in the international media, and the signed intervention of US Secretary of State Hillary Clinton in support of the Western resolution against us (her April 4th cable disclosed by Wikileaks), Sri Lanka succeeded in the battle of arguments, because we had accumulated a sufficient stockpile of soft-power through our credible narrative, rational discourse and broad united front. In the decade 2012-2022, Sri Lankan Governments destroyed all that, beginning with my removal six weeks after our diplomatic victory of 2009, which was never repeated.

Q: But, we have not seen any substantive presentation from the government side denying the so-called genocide charge of some parties. Why?

A: There should have been an internationally credible, domestic accountability mechanism and process as recommended by the LLRC, the Paranagama commission report – authored by Sir Desmond de Silva—but this was never done. Significantly, even Ranil and Mangala buried the Desmond de Silva report, which had an annexure authored by the former head of the British SAS which completely demolished the allegations of a policy of premeditated war crimes on the part of the Sri Lankan military.

Q: Do you think we are losing the grips in the international community to certain elements in Tamil Diaspora?

A: Sure, but it is not just to, or mainly to, elements in the Tamil Diaspora. We have a considerable portion of world opinion against us. This is not due to the Tamil Diaspora; it is due to the ugly face of the Sri Lankan State under both the Rajapaksas and the Ranil presidency due to the latter's repression of unarmed non-violent Aragalaya activists in a context when the Aragalaya restored Sri Lanka's image in the global media and through it in the eyes of the world.

Q: What should be the role of our diplomats and their subordinates to overcome prevailing challenges in the country?

A: Our professional diplomats are doing their best though some Gotabaya appointees especially in a crucial place like Geneva, presented an ugly, truculent image. Their personality and discourse were all wrong. The real problem is with our foreign policy. Without a correct foreign policy which I define as one that goes back at least to Lakshman Kadirgamar and then moves forward from there, you cannot sustain a successful diplomacy.

Q: There was an interesting interview published by Indian media with Milinda Moragoda, the high commissioner of Sri Lanka to India, where he says, "New Delhi's support to Sri Lanka was without "condition" and the package was "extremely flexible". Any thoughts, can you offer us?

A: The problem I have is not with India's support to us, which has been most valuable. It is what successive Sri Lankan administrations have sought to use and misuse India's support for. For the last decade, Sri Lanka has not had a correct foreign policy, which crucially entails a correct India policy. Our India policy has to be the cornerstone of our foreign policy and diplomacy and must be guided by our national interest but it has not been so at any time in the postwar period. Instead, it has been guided by narrow, selfish factors. India rightly takes care of its interests, but we don't similarly take care of ours.

Q: A few incidents recently reported I would like to recall, first, arbitrary scraping of the tender of a project awarded to China due to India's objection; second, for the first time in History India's Minister urged Sri Lanka on an open platform to conduct the elections without any further due and ensure the rights of Tamil speakers; third, Indian mission in Colombo and Jaffna directly influenced the Universities especially the Jaffna University not to sign MOUs with Chinese University impacting the academic freedom. We find it quite contrary to what Mr. Moragoda tells. Your take, please.

A: We have lacked balance and a clear strategic vision of our national interest.

Q: However, Sri Lanka is gearing up for much-delayed local elections. What do you think?

A: If the local election is not held on schedule there will be an uncontrollable chain reaction of social explosions. July 1983, two civil wars and a foreign intervention were all after and due to the postponement of imminent parliamentary elections through a fraudulent and coercive referendum in December 1982. Conversely, we began to emerge from that crisis through the Provincial Council, Presidential and Parliamentary elections of 1988-1989. Elections are the solution not the problem. Postponement of elections is the problem, not the solution.

Q: 13A mantra again on the edge of politics. President Wickremesinghe reaffirmed his willingness to implement the 13th amendment fully. Is it the right time to do it? And do you agree with the way the President is going to implement this?

A: I have always supported the 13th amendment and its implementation, but the modalities, timing and sequencing of full implementation can only be deliberated upon in a triangular discussion between an elected President, a newly elected Parliament and elected Provincial Councils. It will be disastrous if it is undertaken by a president without a popular mandate, a Parliament that has forfeited its popular mandate by doing the exact opposite of that mandate, and a Provincial Council system put into a coma! What Ranil is attempting is like trying to perform brain surgery which requires a laser, with a rusty axe instead!

Q: You are supporting Mr. Sajith Premadasa, and you were with his father too. What is the difference you see between the duo? And the mistakes of his father; Do you think Sajith can capture the people's power? Why do you think he is the best man to run this country?

A: Firstly, as for the mistakes of President Premadasa, I see only one: he did not play the same guiding role in the war against the LTTE that he did in the war against the JVP. Though Ranjan Wijeratne and Sirisena Cooray played the directly leading role – the Ops Combine which defeated the barbaric JVP campaign in a few months reported ultimately to Sirisena Cooray—the guiding role, including the sincere search for peace, was Premadasa's. He did not play the same role in the war against the LTTE and did not let Sirisena Cooray do so either. I lobbied hard for him to do so (and have my memos to prove it), but he said "Dayan, after all this is over the Tamil people must see the Presidency as being above the ethnic issue, so I do not want to be directly associated with this and I prefer to let the professional military handle the task without interference". Sadly, he was wrong and I proved correct. That was his only real mistake.

The democratic system, open society and open economy was saved in 1989 by a Premadasa and Premadasa policies. That's what it took. They will have to be saved again, this time, also by a Premadasa and Premadasa policies.

I support Sajith Premadasa because only he has the right mix of policies necessary to save the economy and democracy in this grave existential crisis. What is that mix? It is globally known as "Growth with Equity". President Premadasa had unprecedentedly high achievements with that mix. Few leaders can do both together but he did so. In the Premadasa years we resumed high growth very swiftly, had high levels of foreign direct investment, rapid export-led decentralized industrialization, a very active Stock Market while simultaneously we had many programs of social upliftment such as Janasaviya, Free School Uniforms, Free Mid-day Meals for school children, and overall a reduction of absolute and relative poverty and income inequality.

The present government is for economic contraction, not expansion—that means low growth, which is disastrous.

The JVP-JJB's policy manifesto is firmly opposed to the Open Economy and globalization – not just neoliberalism, which we should all oppose—and without the open economy and globalization you cannot have high growth.

The centre-right neoliberal economists are for high growth but reject simultaneous high equity as undesirable or impossible. If you have high growth but low equity you will have a revolution!

Throughout the world, only a Social Democratic policy paradigm has a chance of ensuring high growth and greater social equity simultaneously. For 35 years I have been a convinced Social Democrat, even when I was an underground left activist.

In Sri Lanka, only Sajith Premadasa – not even the JVP-JJB— has committed to a Social Democratic paradigm, and he has the advantage of having inherited and absorbed a proven success story of such a social democratic developmental paradigm, i.e., that of his father Ranasinghe Premadasa.

Sajith is a relatively young leader who has the best combination of a good Western education and exposure to the world, with compassionate interventionism on behalf of the majority of the people.

What is the difference between Sajith and his father, you asked; It is the same difference as between my father and me. That difference is best encapsulated in the reply given by the legendary business magnate N.U. Jayawardene (Dr Lal Jayawardena's father and Milinda Moragoda's maternal grandfather), at his daughter-in-law Prof Kumari Jayawardena's home, to my father whom he regarded with some fondness. The question around the dining table had been, "how come NU Jayawardena was an acerbic personality who didn't suffer fools gladly; a rough diamond – while his son Dr Lal Jayawardena was a polite, amiable, tolerant person?" N.U.'s replay had been "well, I am the son of a rest-housekeeper, while he [Lal] is the son of the former Governor of the Central Bank!"

My father Mervyn used to say the same thing when a similar question was asked about him and me. Prof Kumari Jayawardena asked him "Mervyn, see how objective Dayan as a boy, is even about you, his father. He is far more objective than you are. Why can't you be that objective?' Mervyn used to answer: "I am the son of an apothecary, while he [Dayan] is the son of the Editor of the Ceylon Daily News!"

Similarly, Sajith is the English public school and LSE-educated son of an assassinated populist President. Naturally, he and his great-father are somewhat different. Though, both in Sajith's case and mine, vis-à-vis our respective fathers, something that Lee Kuan Yew said is very relevant. When he was asked on the record why he thinks his son can manage Singapore, Lee replied that in his retirement he had been reading a lot of science and that the evidence was conclusive: "80% of one's makeup comes from genetics– transmitted from your parents".

I know for sure that as a first-time diplomat, my successful performance as Ambassador/Permanent Representative in Geneva at a crucial and challenging time in my country's history would not have been possible had I not been the son of Sri Lanka's foremost expert on international affairs and travelled overseas with my parents even when my father covered the 2nd Nonaligned Conference in Cairo under Nasser in September 1964, and I was seven years old.

5

WE ARE EELAM TAMILS

*Neither I nor other Tamil leaders and the Tamil people
hate Sinhala people.*

~

Visuvanathan Rudrakumaran
*Prime minister of the Transnational Government of Tamil
Eelam*

"I MUST state here that our current referendum campaign does not hinge the consent of the Sri Lankan state. A referendum for independence in Kosovo was held without the approval of Serbia. Sri Lanka will not become an economically viable country without a political resolution to the demands of Eelam Tamils," Visuvanathan Rudrakumaran a New York-based Attorney who served as the legal advisor to the Liberation Tigers of Tamil Eelam, told in this interview.

While recalling the memories of slain LTTE leader Velupillai Prabhakaran, he says that "his vision, his dedication, his determination, his passion, his resilience, are always with us."

Rudrakumaran is the prime minister of the Transnational Government of Tamil Eelam which is a transnational organisation among the Sri Lankan Tamil diaspora which aims to establish Tamil Eelam, in the North-East of Sri Lanka. This interview is a part of our series of interviews with noted minds in Tamil Diaspora. The Government of Sri Lanka, recently, renewed its request in which they invited members of the Tamil Diaspora for political and social cohabitation.

Following are the excerpts of the interview;

Question: Rudra, it has been a long time since we last communicated. Thank you for taking the time to sit with us. What latest updates can you offer us on your organization TGTE?

Answer: Our main political program is that the Eelam Tamils, as a distinct Nation, have the right to self-determination and they should decide their political future through a referendum.

Today this vision is gaining acceptance in the international community. As you know, many former presidents, former UN undersecretaries and prominent academics regularly participate in our functions.

Our viewpoint is also finding resonance amidst the Tamil domestic leadership, despite the oppressive military environment and threat posed by the Sixth Amendment, which penalizes peaceful advocacy for an independent state. I also would like to highlight the fact that in a letter sent by the Tamil parliamentarians to the UN High Commissioner for Human Rights dated August 9th, 2022, have called for the repeal of the Sixth Amendment.

We will be soon filing papers with the registrar of the International Criminal Court acceding to the jurisdiction of the ICC in the state of Tamil Eelam. Our accession is based on the fact that the de jure state of Tamil Eelam exists. As you know, the Tamils did not consent to the 1972 as well as the 1978 constitution- our argument is premised on the international legal concept of reversion to sovereignty. In this connection, I would also like to state that the former UN high commissioner Al Hussain called upon the Sri Lankan state to accede to the Rome statute.

I would like to mention that the continued proscription by the Sri Lankan government of the TGTE, which is committed to establish the state of Tamil Eelam through democratic and diplomatic means, is testimony to our effectiveness in the pursuit of our goal.

Q: We heard that your father was a government servant who worked as the Mayor of Jaffna from 1979 to 1983 and passed away in 2020. What legacy did he leave for you to pursue?

A: My father was not a government servant. He was a successful criminal lawyer. He firmly believed that Tamils can live with security and dignity only in an independent Tamil state. He quit practicing law in 1983, since he refused to take oath expressing allegiance to the Sixth Amendment of the constitution. I would also like to point out, when he was the mayor of Jaffna, he refused to receive the then Prime Minister Mr. R. Premadasa. Honesty, sincerity, hard work, commitment to the cause, and commitment to the people, are the hallmarks of his legacy.

Q: Do you recognize yourself as the successor of slain LTTE leader Velupillai Prabhakaran?

A: I do not consider myself as the successor of the Tamil national leader. I believe that no one can be a successor to our national leader. However, I feel I have a moral and political obligation to contribute effectively to the struggle. The Tamil national leader has elevated the Tamil struggle to the international plane and made the Tamil national question an international issue. His achievement/contribution and vision in the realization of Tamil aspirations for an independent state will guide us in moving forward to the end. Our national leader once said that the mode of our struggle might change, but not the goal. We will move forward with democratic and diplomatic means to achieve our goal. The fact that Sri Lanka continues to remain a racist, ethnocratic state only strengthens our resolve.

Q: Do you miss him?

A: His vision, his dedication, his determination, his passion, his resilience, are always with us.

Q: Let us consider the preliminary document prepared by the Advisory Committee of TGTE where you have reaffirmed that Mr. S J V Chelvanayagam is "Eelam Gandhi". Do you believe in non-violence?

A: I strongly believe in Peoples' Power. As I mentioned in the answer to the earlier question, we have adopted a non-violent path to achieve our goal. I would like to point out the tradition of sacrifice by Thileeban and Annai Poopathi who also adopted a non-violent mode of struggle.

Q: What mistakes did the LTTE make?

A: The LTTE was committed to the Tamil cause that was not well matched with the interest of international powers. It can be described as a geopolitical conflict. Between the thirst of Tamils for an independent and sovereign state and the interest of the existing international powers. The reason for the way the war ended in 2009 was that the big regional and global powers did not want a new power center in the Indian Ocean. The powers did not want to make a change in the power structure and balance of power in South Asia and in the Indian Ocean. Given the present collusion between China and Sri Lanka, as demonstrated by the Hambonthota 99 years lease, the arrival of the Chinese submarine in 2014 and the arrival of Yuan Wang 5 last month, that position will surely change in the days ahead.

Q: The same preliminary report of your Advisory Committee lamented the plight of Muslims in Sri Lanka and advocated a secular state. But we don't see any Buddhist or Islamic representatives in your top committee of TGTE. Why?

A: prominent Sinhala human rights activist, Dr. Brian Senewiratne who happens to be a relative of the former Sri Lankan President Chandrika Kumaratunga, has been a prominent member of the TGTE Senate. In 2016, we recognized his contribution to the human rights of Tamils and gave him a "Lifetime Commitment Award". In our Freedom Charter, promulgated with the participation of more than 100,000 people, rather than playing with words like in the Sri Lankan constitution, we stated in article 14 of the Freedom Charter that "Tamil, Sinhala, and English shall be the official languages of Tamil Eelam.

In the Freedom Charter, we explicitly recognized the distinct identity of the Muslims. Moreover, unlike Sri Lanka, which places Buddhism as the foremost religion, article 7 of our

Freedom Charter states that Tamil Eelam shall be a secular state and no religion shall be given foremost place in Tamil Eelam. I must also say that a Sri Lankan Muslim academic also participated in the conference promulgating the Freedom Charter. We are also contemplating having a seminar with the Muslim community regarding our Tamil Eelam referendum campaign.

Q: You strongly believe that the only way Sri Lankan Tamils can protect their rights is to create a separate Tamil homeland. This position can be understood by assessing Sri Lanka's past records that you have no real intention to solve the problems of the common men and women in the North East but lag behind the unrealistic goal. Correct us if we are wrong.

A: I would like to first categorically deny the identity of our people as "Sri Lankan Tamils". We consider ourselves as Eelam Tamils and People of Tamil Eelam. Sri Lanka is a Sinhala, Buddhist, fundamentalist state that has systematically been engaged in structural genocide of Tamil people. An independent sovereign Tamil state is the only solution for safeguarding Tamil people from the genocidal policies and actions of the Sri Lankan state.

In fact, Ms. Michelle Bachelet, the former UN High Commissioner for Human Rights, in her report issued 6 September 2022 expressed concerns about "the trend towards majoritarianism… former president Rajapaksha actively promoted a Sinhala Buddhist majoritarian ideology with the support of the military and Buddhist monks."

As the East Timor president and noble laureate, Dr Jose Ramos Horta at the fifth Mullivaikal Memorial lecture on May 18th 2020, stated "The ruling Sri Lankan state must ask themselves why Tamils are actively seeking a separate state and acknowledge what may be going wrong."

The scuttling of the P-TOMS by the Sri Lankan judiciary and the utter failure of the provincial council clearly demonstrates that until a political resolution is reached, economic development cannot happen.

I also take issue with your characterization that Tamil Eelam is an unrealistic goal. In fact, the continuation of Sri Lanka as an ethnocratic state, ruled in perpetuity by racist Sinhala elites is an unrealistic goal. The growing recognition of the fact within the international community that the Tamils were subjected to genocide accelerates the process of realising our independence. Law and morality dictate that as a form of remedial justice in order to ensure "Never Again", the formation of an independent state is the proper form of remedial justice.

I also would like to point out that given the fact that the island of Sri Lanka is situated in a strategically important place in the Indian Ocean, and it is the Tamils who inhabit two-thirds of the coastline, the evolving power dynamics should also be noted in this connection. As you know, since 1990, more than 30 states have been established. We believe that history is moving in the direction of Tamil people achieving their highest political aspiration.

Q: Do you hate Sinhalese? When was the last time you communicated with a Sinhala Buddhist?

A: Neither I nor other Tamil leaders and the Tamil people hate Sinhala people. Our struggle is against the chauvinistic and genocidal Sri Lankan state. I provide legal representation for many Sinhalese here in the US. Some of my Sinhala clients even seek my advice for their family matters. Some of my Sinhala clients have also stated, during the current economic crisis, that the reign over the whole country should have been given to Mr. Velupillai Pirabaharan. In their opinion he would have governed the country with honesty and discipline. I think you should check my reputation among the Sinhala and Muslim working-class diaspora in New York city.

Q: How do you read about the present economic meltdown in Sri Lanka?

A: The present economic meltdown is primarily caused by the atrocity crimes committed against the Tamils and the continued military subjugation of Tamils. The militarization of the country contributes heavily to the present economic catastrophe. The UN high commissioner, in her report dated September 6th 2022, stated that "the Defense Ministry was allocated – 354 billion Sri Lankan rupees (US $1.86 billion) which accounted for 15% of the total government expenditure making it the highest allocated sector in 2022".

Coupled with the above, the disrespect for the rule of law for decades has enabled corruption to go so deep that it has destroyed the Sri Lankan economy. Another related factor in more recent times has been the reliance on China for high interest loans for useless projects. The Covid pandemic and the war in Ukraine only tipped over a thoroughly rotten system.

Q: How can you support Sri Lankans to overcome the current challenge?

A: I take this question as how Tamils can support and overcome the current catastrophe. As we have stated earlier there first needs to be a political solution to the Tamil national question by holding a referendum to decide the political future of Eelam Tamils. I must state here that our current referendum campaign does not hinge the consent of the Sri Lankan state. A referendum for independence in Kosovo was held without the approval of Serbia.

Sri Lanka will not become an economically viable country without a political resolution to the demands of Eelam Tamils. Such a solution will bring peace and prosperity for everyone. It will also motivate the Eelam Tamil Diaspora to invest in Sri Lanka also.

Q: The President has invited the Tamil Diaspora to be part of rebuilding Sri Lanka. We believe it's a great opportunity for you to put your feet on the ground and do something substantive. Would you like to communicate with the government?

A: I think the answers given to previous questions are relevant to this question too. When I left Sri Lanka in 1982, my intention was to finish my one-year master's degree and return to Sri Lanka. After the 1983 racial pogrom I felt that based on my credentials, I could contribute to the liberation of our people more effectively by being outside. Given the fact, there's no space for Tamils for justice or to articulate their political aspirations fully, it is imperative for me to continue to stay outside the island. I am sure I will return and put 'my feet on the ground' and that will be on the soil of an independent Tamil Eelam.

6

TAMIL DIASPORA IS THE PRODUCT OF DOWNRIGHT FAILURES

I have no hesitation in saying the failure of LTTE was its own making.

~

Rajasingham Jayadevan
Secretary, Eelapatheeswarar Aalayam

TALKING about President Wickremesinghe's invitation to Tamil Diaspora to rebuild the country he says that is a kneejerk request without consideration of the wider issues involved. This appeal can be only responded if a far-reaching package is offered to the expats by the government, he says.

The government must realise, that the Tamil diaspora is the product of its downright failures and must go as far as to revise its failures in a substantive way, Rajasingham Jayadevan said in an interview with me. Speaking from his residence in London, Jayadevan did not hesitate to recall his past experiences with the LTTE saying that the "failure of LTTE was its own making. LTTE's fundamental mistake was to move away from a just struggle of the people to a struggle for the redemption of traditional homelands."

Mr Jayadevan is a social worker, writer, and influential voice of the Tamil Diaspora based in London. He is the Secretary, Eelapatheeswarar Aalayam, and Non Resident Tamils of Sri Lanka and private sector Finance Director.

"One needs to deep think whether Sri Lanka has the capacity to reform its path in a broader sense," he suggested.

Excerpts of the interview;

Question: Jaya, thank you for joining me today. Let us briefly know your experiences before and after your captivity by the LTTE. True, LTTE is no longer active but we are sure you still have a strong memory that you would like to recall.

Answer: It is seventeen years since my incarceration by the LTTE. My experience post release was inhumane and calculated campaign against me for publicising my experience without fear. The brand name of 'traitor' was bestowed on me, and it was an experience worse than my captivity itself in Vanni. Friends became foes and foes became friends. Their campaign of harassment was relentless and all and sundry in anonymity. They campaigned to dehumanise me and my family in a disrespectful manner. Determination and fearlessness strived me through and I am whom I am in my onerous progression to best serve the suffering people in the post war Sri Lanka.

I have no hesitation in saying the failure of LTTE was its own making. LTTE's fundamental mistake was to move away from a just struggle of the people to a struggle for the redemption of traditional homelands. People became victims to its hegemonic gun hoe mechanism to establish territorial control and the LTTE also failed to realise the fast-changing local and international realities on terrorism and suppression of civil wars. Over thirty years of war saw generational thinking change and the war inflicted untold suffering and pain for the people and LTTE could not preside over anymore when the Tamil feelings having negative towards the LTTE and further because of the untold misery burdened on them by the government forces.

I am very active and heavily engaged in post-war regeneration work in Sri Lanka. In the progressing decay in Sri Lanka, post war reconciliation and revival are facing hammer blow experience.

Q: At least three governments came to power after the end of the Civil War. Certain areas such as infrastructure and other social welfare facilities like education were tremendously improved in North and East since then. But we still hear the same criticism against the central government. We would like to know your take.

A: The post war effort of the government to regenerate the North and East has been bare minimum. It failed to harness meaningful resources for the regeneration of North and East of Sri Lanka. There was no laudable post war plan or consensus politics or even reparation for the victims of the war to revive their lives. Much needed international support was overtly disregarded as the government remained exposed of war crimes charges which is continuing to burgeon the country – a factor influencing the present socio-economic decay the country is facing at present.

The true cause of the war is the anti-Tamil Standardization Policy of the government of Sirimavo Bandaranaike of the late 1960's. It did collateral damage to the vibrant Tamil community and the aftermath was the painful history that is still impacting the country. Whatever the government facilitated post-war efforts are seen as just sweeteners and not substantive programme of work. The government does not have the resources, or the war weary Tamil community is capacitated to respond to needs on their own on the issues facing them.

Q: Tell us about your social project in the post-war period. How did you enable funds and what are the challenges you face?

A: I was a regular visitor to Sri Lanka, though last few years have constrained me due to Covid pandemic and my personal circumstances. I am heavily involved in post-war socio-economic revival work through the charity Eelapatheeswarar Aalayam – UK, I represent. Guided by my brother Late Dr R Narendran we initiated his unique idea of post war village development work. We adopted the downtrodden Pulayaveli Village in Chengaladi in Batticaloa. My bother gave us the much-needed energy to engage heavily in infrastructural development work. His sudden demise a year later in 2017 numbed us all, but his perseverance and determination laid the foundation for us to proceed further. It was uphill task as distance of 5,500 miles between London and Colombo was serious challenge for us. It has been day to day remote control management work. My day starts at 3.00am and with my other commitments in London the charity was able to build good working relationship that helped to proceed further to substantially develop the village.

The devotees and well-wishers of the temple charity provided the funds for the costly work. As we progressed, we earned the goodwill of the people for our effective management and accountability. We are content that the very trust we earned with the diaspora community with our transparent engagement, is helping us to widen our work programme is in a greater scale.

I will be failing if I do not reflect my note of caution in such heavy engagement by anyone. The challenge in managing such broad-based programme has its downfalls as Sri Lanka has created a society that is habitual takers and would not doers they do not understand meaning of reciprocal engagement with their minimum contribution in return. The beggar bowl culture of yearning for handouts has weakened the capacity of the people to progress energetically.

Q: How do you see the present situation in Sri Lanka?

A: The present situation is dire. When international credit rating agency Moody's downgraded the credit worthiness of Sri Lanka three years ago, the GoSL did not consider their findings seriously to address the failures responsibly. Instead, Sri Lanka went on the anti- Moody spree to belittle its findings. Following Moody, leading international agencies continued to downgrade Sri Lanka. With their negative assessments and the consequences of Covid-19 pandemic, Sri Lanka paying a heavy price for its failures in its economic management. Deep-rooted corruption from the office peons to the President was draining the state resources. Post-war did not witness downsizing of the military and the bloated unproductive state sector employment. Instead of stretching their hands to the IMF and other reputable international actors, Sri Lanka was playing ping pong in the international arena. Sri Lanka's hostile stance on war crimes claims by the UNHRC is another factor influencing the decay faced by the country.

Sri Lanka, since independence, has destroyed the four supportive pillars of its foundation. The Burgers, plantation Tamils, indigenous Tamils, and the Muslims were systematically marginalised to establish outright majoritarian rule. The whole political mechanism has now crumbled with the worst form of governance inhibiting Sri Lanka. In Sri Lanka, all and sundry can become president and legislators and it is norm to tamper with constitution for petty parochial reasons. The nation never produced a national leader to transform Sri Lanka, and election of nationalists have caused untold misery for nation. Mahinda Rajapakse had the golden opportunity to become a national leader with the defeat of the LTTE, but he too was part of the marathon race to extend the curse of nationalist politics.

One need to deep think whether Sri Lanka has the capacity to reform its path in broader sense. It is endless pit to find an answer as the malice inhibiting is so entrenched that and any effort for real transformation will be a dream in Alice in Wonderland. The present economic decay is giving the right message for the need for broad based responsible governance. One wonders how long this will merit when belly aching hunger is addressed.

Q: Sri Lanka cannot effort another armed conflict, but many political commentators are worrying the current social upheaval may lead to an unprecedented violent conflict. How can you and Sri Lankans expatriates help maintain social normalcy?

A: Sri Lanka brewing for social unrest in an unprecedented scale if substantive efforts are not made to bring normally in its economic performance. Sri Lankan expatriate is a vibrant resource and expecting them to help redeem the malaise is daydream. The non-resident community too is going through transformation as the marathon sticks are being passed fast to the next generation who have very little engagement with Sri Lanka. The president of Sri Lanka has made some proposals for diaspora engagement, and these are kneejerk requests without consideration of wider issues involved. His appeal can be only responded if far-reaching package is offered to the expats by the government. The government must realise, the Tamil diaspora is the product of its downright failures and must go as far as to revise its failures in a substantive way for them to engage positively in Sri Lanka.

7

UNMASKING
WESTERN HYPOCRISY

Russia is an independent country, and the US does not like independent countries.

~

Levan S. Dzhagaryan
Russian Ambassador to Sri Lanka

RUSSIAN Ambassador to Sri Lanka Levan S. Dzhagaryan emphasizes the importance of learning and respecting the true history of the countries we work with, as well as the need for open dialogue and modesty in diplomatic interactions.

I had the opportunity to conduct an exclusive interview with the Russian Ambassador to Sri Lanka, Levan S. Dzhagaryan, at the Russian Embassy in Colombo just a few days after he assumed his duties. The interview covered a range of topics including the longstanding relationship between Sri Lanka and Russia, the current state of bilateral relations, the de-dollarization campaign of Global South, and the Ambassador's message to foreign diplomats.

Ambassador Dzhagaryan shared his thoughts and insights on these important issues, providing valuable perspectives on the challenges and opportunities facing Sri Lanka and the wider international community. The interview provided a unique opportunity to gain deeper insights into the perspectives of one of the most senior Russian diplomats in the region, and sheds light on the current state of relations between Sri Lanka and Russia, as well as the broader geopolitical dynamics shaping the world today.

Levan S. Dzhagaryan has an extensive diplomatic career that includes working in various regions around the world, including the Middle East. He has served as a diplomat for over three decades, beginning his career in 1987. He has worked in Iran, Afghanistan, and other countries in the region, gaining invaluable experience in dealing with complex political and diplomatic situations.

In the late 1980s, Dzhagaryan served as a diplomat in Afghanistan during the Soviet military presence in Afghanistan, a period of intense conflict and political turmoil. This experience provided him with a unique perspective on international relations, conflict resolution, and the importance of dialogue and cooperation between nations.

Read the excerpts from the interview;

Question [A]: Mr. Ambassador, thank you very much for accepting our request. Let's start this interview with your assessment of the ongoing conflict between Russia and Ukraine. How is the situation there now?

Answer [A]: This is not a conflict between Ukraine and Russia, but rather a conflict between Russia and Western countries, particularly the United States of America. What we are expecting is for Ukraine to announce that it is a NATO country. Then they can officially deploy their forces, which they are currently doing unofficially, near the Russian border by forcing a direct threat.

Imagine if Russia deployed our missiles close to the United States, as happened in Cuba in 1962, and everyone knows what happened. Now the same thing is being done by the United States in our border countries. How on earth can that be justified? When they do it, it is justifiable, but when others do it to ensure their borders, it is not acceptable and is called an "unprovoked war" or "invasion." This is nothing but a double standard.

Q: You are pointing at the West, but the more the crisis drags on, the more people suffer. Responsible parties must take immediate steps to solve this problem. Do you have anything in mind in terms of conflict resolution?

A: To resolve this crisis, China is playing a significant and remarkable role. To cease the ongoing violence and find a lasting solution, China last month proposed a 12-point peace plan. Some provisions of this plan that may lay a foundation for peace negotiations, but Ukraine is continuing to play a hoodwink as they cannot decide by themselves. Ukraine is obviously a puppet government. They are under American and certain European countries' control. Ukrainians are not decision-makers. Everything they do depends on Washington. Therefore, they are afraid of a ceasefire, as a ceasefire would benefit unarmed civilians. What they want is more suffering for civilians and for the war to continue. These manipulators don't want peace, and if they continue like this, we have no alternative but to continue the war and upgrade it into a full-scale war.

Q: If you can talk about the geopolitical landscape in this crisis, what is the biggest threat to Russia at the moment?

A: The current geopolitical scenario is a threat to our sovereignty and independence. Russia is an independent country, and the US does not like independent countries. That is why they are trying to undermine China. The new world order is giving us an opportunity to understand who we are and how the West has bullied us. The threat Russia is facing is not an isolated threat. This is exactly what the Global South is facing at this moment. That is why the Global South is coming together.

Q: You have repeatedly stated that Russia is unfairly targeted by the West. Can you explain your perspective on this issue?

A: Indeed, we firmly believe that Russia is unfairly targeted by the West. We have always been willing to cooperate with any country on an equal footing. In the past, we have had strong relationships with charismatic political leaders in the West who understood Russia's integrity. We worked together while protecting mutual respect and sensitivity. One example is Germany, where Russia helped to prosper its economy. However, some countries have recently blown up energy pipelines, attempting to blame Russia, but their efforts have been unsuccessful. We have urged the UN Security Council to set up a working group to investigate this crime, but it is being refused. Everyone knows who is behind this attack, and it was not simply a group in Ukraine, but a sophisticated attack. Therefore, after the incident, President Biden, Under Secretary Nuland, and others shared their joys. It is evident that Americans were using trade with European countries to promote their trade, and this is precisely what has happened. As a result, Europeans are now forced to purchase expensive LNG, and they will soon realize who their true enemy is.

Q: Many countries abstained from voting on the Russian resolution at the UN Security Council on Nord Stream Sabotage. Can you comment on this?

A: Yes, only three countries stood in favor of our resolution. Other countries refrained from voting due to enormous pressure from the United States and its allies. We have to ask, if these countries had nothing to do with this international terror act of sabotaging the pipeline, why are they afraid of conducting an impartial investigation? Why won't they allow Russians to be a part of this investigation?

Q: The West has responded to your allegations by saying that they are unproven. How do you react to this?

A: If our allegations are unproven, then we are willing to participate and cooperate in an investigation. However, they have continued to deny our demands for an impartial investigation. This attack is an act of state terrorism and shameful inhumanity. They have no right to blame other countries. The country that created ISIS has no right whatsoever to criticize other countries. President Trump even publicly told Hilary Clinton, when she was Secretary of State, "You should be rewarded by ISIS because you have created them."

Q: Let's talk about your role as a Russian diplomat. You served as the Russian Ambassador to Iran before your assignment here in Colombo. What do you see as the biggest threat Iran is facing today, and how can Russia help address it?

A: Iran is a beautiful and rich country with friendly people. However, since 1979, Iran has been suffering from unfairly targeted sanctions imposed by the US and EU. Despite this, Iran has managed to create a strong economy. I particularly saw that Iranian youth are true patriots and are well-versed in mathematics and sciences, which is a huge national potential. But the US is always poking Iran and trying their best to destabilize the country using different tools. Certain media outfits and social groups funded by the West situated abroad are trying to defame Iran and topple the government. The West can't tolerate when there is an independent country. As a true friend with historic roots, Russia maintains a strong relationship with Iran, and we have mutual respect for each other. China's move to normalize relationships with other Middle Eastern countries, including Iran, is significant, and I hope we can work towards strong relationships with other Arab countries, particularly Turkey and Syria.

Q: The interesting point is the US doesn't have a physical mission in Iran, but during the Obama administration, they started nuclear negotiations. How do you see this?

A: Switzerland is keeping a special unit to maintain the Iran-US relationship, and there are a few other Western missions operating in Tehran. At the time, they were very cooperative, which ultimately resulted in a good deal. But later, it turned into a blunt attempt to interfere with Iran's internal affairs.

Q: The Iraq intervention is now 20 years old, and the crisis in the Middle East continues. Do you see any light at the end of the tunnel in the region?

A: Many issues need to be solved, and as a diplomat, I'm optimistic about it. However, the Iraq intervention by the US and its allies, like in many other countries, is a gross violation of international laws and conventions, as well as the United Nations Charter. Just like how they destroyed Iraq, Americans are destroying Syria. The presence of American troops in Syria is not only unnecessary but also a gross violation of the country's sovereignty. Who invited them to Syria? Nobody. They are just there to loot, yes; loot the natural resources from Syria. Our demand is to withdraw the American troops from Syria quickly and start a dialogue with the government headed by President Asad. As far as I understand, the President is ready for a dialogue with opposition groups. I think all parties should come to a compromise to end this brutal crisis instigated by the West.

Q: But at the same time, those regimes, be it Syria, Iraq, Libya, or elsewhere, are blamed for serious violations of human rights?

A: What are human rights? It is a well-formulated tool for double standards. Americans have a lot of problems inside their country; if they are concerned about human rights, they should solve their issues at home first before dictating to other countries on how to protect human rights. They turn a blind eye to certain countries of their choice but attack other independent countries for not bowing down to their dictations. Look at Latvia and Estonia; many Russians are there without identities. Does the West talk about that? No, because they maintain friendship with them. What about the killing of Darya Dugina by Ukrainian assassins? Do any "human rights nations" or any human rights protection and promotion organizations talk about it? Not at all. Their hypocrisy is crystal clear. Those who deny the actions of the Ukrainian government are not persecuted, and those who speak against it are. In my opinion, whenever the Western allegations on human rights come up, first see their ulterior motives and track records, then you can see the double standards and hypocrisy there. What you have to be careful of is not allowing those hypocrites to interfere in your internal affairs.

Q: Do you think, in this situation, the Global South moving forward to establish a multipolar world is a realistic dream?

A: It is indeed realistic, and more and more countries in the Global South are coming together after centuries of bullying and undermining. The West has deceived us with their lies right from the beginning; how can we trust them? The United Nations itself rules out that Americans violated international laws and conventions. If they start bragging about human rights protection and promotion, my message is very clear: please stand up and see yourself in the mirror. In Syria, my message is even clearer: "Yankees, go home!"

Q: Well, give us your take on the recent visit by Chinese President Xi Jinping.

A: We are very happy about this significant move. We are not a military alliance. We don't force threats to anyone else, but we stand for securing our borders and sovereignty. We are focused on the humanitarian field, more importantly, the economy of each other.

Q: However, the US Dollar is still dominating the global economy.

A: We must work towards getting rid of the US dollar as the dominant currency. Our priorities are to establish an undisrupted supply chain, prevent external meddling in internal affairs, and achieve independent economic sustainability. The de-dollarization campaign is gaining momentum and trades between countries using local currencies are increasing. Russia, China, Iran, India, and Saudi Arabia have all seen success in these trades. The era of US dollar dominance is coming to an end, and these are positive signs. I hope the Global South will become even more united and strong to face future challenges.

Q: But whenever this discourse on de-dollarization comes to light, there will be a Western-sponsored war that breaks out. For instance, when Saddam Hussein started selling oil to Europe using European currencies, the United States bombed Iraq. When Muammar al-Qaddafi of Libya started selling oil for gold, the United States bombed Libya. I'm afraid the same scenario might be repeated soon to divert attention from the deepening financial crisis in the West.

A: It is indeed possible. As you correctly point out, Western powers may create a tipping point to divert attention from their domestic issues and focus on external enemies. It is ironic that most of the time, the "external enemy" is also created by them. For instance, in the case of Libya, it was a transit point connecting the West and Africa. Muammar al-Qaddafi was a nice man to the West and bribed many Western political leaders. Ultimately, he paid the price, but at what cost?

Q: With complex and interconnected challenges, how can a country like Sri Lanka work together with Russia and other like-minded countries? You know Sri Lanka is under many obligations over its current financial predicament.

A: I understand that the situation in Sri Lanka is crucial and serious. We are pursuing a very balanced position on Sri Lanka, in terms of our bilateral relationships and other international issues, including the Ukraine crisis. We hope Sri Lanka will be able to settle its domestic problems soon. As the Russian ambassador, I would like to reaffirm that we do not interfere in the internal affairs of Sri Lanka. Our message is that Sri Lanka is rising by itself and overcoming challenges, and I don't think anyone has the right to lecture Sri Lanka on what to do.

I may sound like I'm extremely anti-American, but I am not. American people are a grateful people, and they have created a very strong nation with many talented people in many subjects. We respect the American people, but we cannot agree with the aggressive and provocative actions of the United States government, including the Congress.

Q: Sri Lanka and Russia have maintained longstanding relationships since the USSR era. How do you plan to strengthen our bilateral relationship during your time as the Russian ambassador to Sri Lanka?

A: As a new ambassador to South Asia, I have proposed several projects to the Sri Lankan government that can take our relationship to the next level. Although our focus is currently on Ukraine and defeating its puppet regime, we are also looking to expand our agricultural and trade ties while encouraging more Russian tourists to visit Sri Lanka.

Q: Finally, as a senior Russian diplomat, what message do you have for foreign diplomats?

A: My message is simple: Learn, learn, and learn. Try to study the true history of the country you are working on and be modest. Be open to dialogue and listen to each other. While dedicating yourself to your motherland, also try to love and respect the country you are working in. Arrogance or the desire to interfere in the internal affairs of a country will only complicate the situation and lead you nowhere.

8

THE CIA'S LEGACY

KEY EVENTS THAT SHAPED AMERICAN INTELLIGENCE

In intelligence terms, the challenge is to know how and when to change.

~

Rhodri Jeffreys-Jones
Historian and former political candidate

THE US projects an image of a country devoted to the rule of law, but certain actions of the CIA make that seem like hypocrisy.

In his most recent book, *A Question of Standing*, historian and former political candidate Rhodri Jeffreys-Jones takes a close look at the first 75 years of the Central Intelligence Agency (CIA) and the recognizable events that have shaped its history. In a recent interview with our diplomatic affairs editor, Jeffreys-Jones discussed the ongoing relevance of the CIA and the vital intelligence function it continues to perform in a wide variety of situations.

Born in Wales in 1942, Jeffreys-Jones boasts an impressive academic background, including a B.A. from UCW Aberystwyth and a Ph.D. from Cambridge University. He has held numerous postdoctoral fellowships and research awards, including from the Leverhulme Trust, the British Academy, and the Fulbright Programme. For many years, Jeffreys-Jones was a Professor of History at the University of Edinburgh and the chair of its Department of History, the largest department of any description in a non-collegiate UK university.

Jeffreys-Jones is the author of five edited books and twelve more books as the sole author, including The American Left: Its Impact on Politics and Society since 1900 and The Nazi Spy Ring in America: Hitler's Agents, the FBI, and the Case that Stirred the Nation. He is also the founder and former chair of the Scottish Association for the Study of America, where he currently serves as honorary president.

Read on for Jeffreys-Jones's insights into the CIA's past, present, and future

Question [Q]: What inspired you to write A Question of Standing, and what do you hope readers will take away from it?

Answer (A): My interest in espionage arose from an earlier concern with labour spies. One day, my friend Draguliub Zivojinovic suggested, in the light of that concern, that I look at the papers of English novelist Somerset Maugham, who, it transpired, spied on the Bolsheviks in St Petersburg on behalf of the UK and USA. It sparked my long-term interest in intelligence history. More recently, with the approach of the 75th anniversary of the CIA, I noticed there was no up to date survey of the agency's history. I thought there was an opportunity to meet that need and at the same time to correct what in my view seemed to be certain misconceptions. The book is organized chronologically and around particular themes that most readers will recognize, such as Cuba, Iran, and the killing of Osama bin Laden. I hope readers will take away a better understanding of topics in which they are already interested, and take the opportunity to develop a broader view, too.

Q: The CIA has been a controversial agency throughout its history. What, in your opinion, are some of the key moments or decisions that have shaped its reputation?

A: There has been a tendency to take a US-centered view of this matter. According to this perspective, the CIA's reputation for anticipating events had proceeded from one trough to another. Failure to predict when the Soviets would achieve atomic capability, to anticipate the Yom Kippur War, and to forestall 9/11, are legendary. The assumption is that between these events the agency has registered a stream of unknown triumphs, unknown because of the secret nature of the business. On the operational front, too, visible disasters have affected perceptions. The failure of the Bay of Pigs operation to overthrow Fidel Castro in Cuba is an example. There have also been perceived operational triumphs, such as the killing of Bin Laden, an event that inspired a spontaneous gathering of people outside the White House chanting 'CIA! CIA!'

A main argument on my book is that the reputation of the

CIA outside America is a different story. The CIA's overthrow of democratically elected governments in Iran and Guatemala in the 1950s produced an adverse reaction in non-aligned nations and contributed to the USA's loss of a majority in the UN General Assembly. They were disasters masquerading – in the USA – as successes. Outside the USA the Bay of Pigs was a culmination of woes, not (as perceived in the USA) a first-time occurrence.

Q: Your book takes a balanced approach to the CIA, neither celebrating nor condemning its actions. Can you talk more about this approach and how you arrived at it?

A: US and other reviewers of the book comment on my objectivity. My non-partisanship can be explained by the fact that I am neither a US citizen who has grown up unconsciously supportive of American perspectives, nor a citizen of a victim country that has been adversely affected by the CIA's actions, and thus takes an instinctively critical stance.

The point could be made that I am not quite so objective as reviewers say, as I am British, and the UK is a loyal supporter to the USA in international affairs. However, there is a further gloss here. I grew up in a small Celtic country. My native language is Welsh, not English. When kids of my generation went to the cinema in Wales and saw 'Western' movies, we cheered the 'Indians' and booed the US cavalry. Long ago, the Celts were victims of Roman, then Norman, then English imperialism. Even if that is a fading memory, resistance to external domination remains in the blood.

Q: In your view, what is the most important contribution that the CIA has made to US foreign relations over the past 75 years?

A: Restraint. The sober intelligence estimates supplied by civilian analysts in the CIA have helped more than once to enable the USA to step back from the brink of disaster. In the

1950s, the CIA discredited a distorted view of Soviet intentions and capabilities promoted by the military. In the 1970s the agency supplied intelligence that led to a limitation of the nuclear arms race. In the 1980s its reports facilitated the end of the Cold War. In 2007, a famous intelligence finding discredited claims that Iran was constructing nuclear weapons. In all these cases, bloodthirsty militaristic hawks were kept at bay.

Q: How has the role and standing of the CIA changed over time, and what factors have contributed to these changes?

A: One factor is that in times of international tension American citizens rallied to support the CIA, seeing it as a patriotic institution. Conversely, in periods of detente, such as in the 1970s and 1990s, there were press criticisms and congressional investigations. Since 9/11, the picture has changed, and people have post-Cold War priorities. For example, the CIA plunged in Republican voters' esteem when the agency confronted President Trump over the Russian attempt to manipulate the 2016 presidential election. Outside the USA, the drivers of standing have been different. For example, I have never met an American who did not approve of President Obama's decision to kill Bin Laden instead of bringing him to trial. Outside the USA, there are questions about the wisdom and justice of that act, and of the wider policy of assassination by drone.

The domestic standing of the CIA — in the White House, Congress, and public opinion — governs the degree to which it can influence policy. Infractions of civil liberties at home, for example spying on student protesting the Vietnam War, are a sure stimulus to discontent with the CIA. It should be added that the position changed in 2004, when an intelligence reform act reduced the standing of the CIA. After that date, the director of the CIA no longer had the additional job of coordinating the entire intelligence community. That change reflected two events that damaged the standing of the CIA —

its failure to anticipate the 9/11 attack, and its erroneous endorsement of the view that Saddam Hussein's Iraq had weapons of mass destruction — a finding that led to the disastrous US invasion of Iraq that destabilized the Middle East.

Q: One of the chapters in your book focuses on the CIA's involvement in the War on Terror. How do you evaluate the agency's performance in this conflict?

A: Not highly. On the tactical level, the CIA can be superficially effective. For example, it can use technology and sometimes information from informers to identify suspects and to kill them, or to 'render' (i.e. kidnap and deliver) them to interrogation centers. This kind of operation comes at a cost in terms of 'soft diplomacy' as it alienates many who might otherwise by sympathetic with what the US is trying to accomplish. The US projects an image of a country devoted to the rule of law, but certain actions of the CIA make that seem like hypocrisy.

A more fundamental flaw stems from the foreign policy objectives that underpin the CIA's choice of actions. One person's terrorist is another person's patriot, saint, or martyr. Those whom the CIA targets often seem, to the target's sympathizers, to have right on their side. The classic example, one that evokes strong reactions in the overlapping Moslem and Arab worlds, is the Palestinian resistance movement. America's one-sided support of the Israeli government's disregard for Palestinian rights and aspirations has for decades been the single greatest fomenter of international terrorism. To deal with that type of terrorism, policy change is more important than any action the CIA may undertake.

Q: The Intelligence Reform and Terrorism Prevention Act of 2004 is seen as having diminished the CIA's role. Can you talk about the reasons for this and whether you think it was the right decision?

A: The Act seemed to diminish the CIA's role because it implied that the agency had been incompetent in regard to 9/11, and then to weapons of mass destruction. These verdicts diminished faith in the agency and caused demoralization within it. In administrative terms, management of the wider intelligence community (including the FBI, National Security Agency, Defense Intelligence Agency, etc.) passed from the office of the director of the CIA to the office of the newly created Director of National Intelligence (DNI). Important analytical responsibilities shifted to the Council for National Security, which reported in turn to the DNI. It remains to be seen whether the DNI coordinates intelligence better than the CIA. My view is that the arrangement will remain in place until the next intelligence disaster.No-one can convincingly argue that a Pearl Harbor or 9/11 will never again happen. To return to a subtlety in your question, 'seen as having diminished the CIA's role', all is indeed not as it seems. The CIA is still a powerful and essential tool in the USA's national security kit. It has an espionage and analytical capacity that remains indispensable.

Q: Your book defends the CIA's exposure of foreign meddling in US elections. What do you think are the key challenges facing the agency in this area, and how can they be addressed?

A: The CIA's John Brennan warned the Russians in advance that any attempt to meddle in internal US affairs would backfire. Consciously or unconsciously, he may have been thinking of the CIA's own experiences — for examples, the agency's participation in a plot to overthrow the democratic government of Iran in 1953 created a backlash that continues to the present day.

When President Vladimir Putin's surrogates ignored Brennan's advice and secretly tried to discredit Hilary Clinton's bid for the US presidency in 2016, it was with the intention of strengthening the chances of Donald Trump, a declared friend of Russia. But when the CIA exposed the plot, it made it impossible for President Trump, once elected, to enact his dream of more harmonious Russo-American relations. Arguably, Russian enactment of distrust of NATO via the invasion of Ukraine would not have taken place, had Trump succeeded in his foreign policy goal. A cynic might push the argument further and argue that the CIA should have let matter lie.

As things stand, the key challenges now facing the CIA are how to expedite Ukrainian resistance while, at the same time, facilitating a 'back channel' approach to Moscow to try to bring about a return to peace.

Q: Looking to the future, what role do you think the CIA will play in US foreign relations, and what challenges will it face?

A: The CIA will continue to perform a vital intelligence function in a wide variety of situations we can only guess at today. Under the current leadership of President Joe Biden and CIA director William Burns, it would seem that (except for operations no doubt currently underway in Ukraine) the agency has turned a corner and is running fewer undercover action programs. It remains to be seen whether future presidents will have the strength of character to resist taking the apparently easy option of covert action when faced with difficult foreign policy issues.

In intelligence terms, the challenge is to know how and when to change. America was taken by surprise at the time of 9/11 partly because the CIA did not have sufficient foreign-language capacity quickly to translate digital messages emanating from Afghanistan that would have given clues about the attack. But such crises are difficult to foresee. Which languages should CIA specialists learn for the future?

I concur with the warning given by many specialists, that digital threats to national security will become more and more serious. Countering them will take a great deal of technical skill and — a CIA responsibility — counterintelligence. Proportionality needs to be kept in mind. Do you exclude Chinese chip technology at a cost to your communications systems? Would it be better to trade, bearing in mind the economist Adam Smith's axiom that world trade equals world peace? Does trade-dependency always carry an unacceptable risk of blackmail?

Q: Finally, what are you working on next, and what can readers expect from your future writing?

A: I have now returned to my earlier interest in labour espionage. Spying on workers was the economic mainstay of America's ground-breaking Pinkerton National Detective Agency. My near-complete book, Allan Pinkerton: His Life and Legacies, opens with chapters about the agency's founder, who was born in Scotland, where I now reside. The book goes on to discuss the origins of modern surveillance, and the respective merits of public and private police services. Once Georgetown University Press have published that book, my plan is to write a number of shorter pieces on subjects ranging from the origins of US central intelligence to the politics of preserving non-English languages, especially Welsh.

9

UKRAINE STANDS FIRM AGAINST RUSSIAN AGGRESSION

Victory of Ukraine is a victory of a democratic world.

~

Ivan Konovalov
Charge de Affairs, Embassy of Ukraine in the Republic of India

WE ARE fighting for our freedom and independence. we fight against Russia protecting others in Europe from this threat and our partners understand this very well.

During an interview with me at his New Delhi office, Ivan Konovalov, Charge de Affairs a.i. at the Embassy of Ukraine in the Republic of India (concurrently in Sri Lanka), expressed his belief that Ukraine would achieve more victories on the battlefield this spring. He emphasized that the Ukrainian people have never desired to engage in war but were compelled to defend themselves against the aggression of Russia. Konovalov asserted that this conflict is imperialist in nature, indicating that Russia's actions are driven by a desire for territorial expansion and control.

Furthermore, Konovalov stated that the victory of Ukraine would represent a triumph for democracy across the globe, as it would be a victory for the principles of self-determination and the right of nations to decide their own fate. He highlighted the importance of recognizing that the conflict in Ukraine is not merely a regional issue but rather a struggle for values that are fundamental to the democratic world. Ultimately, Konovalov's comments underscore the ongoing importance of supporting Ukraine in its efforts to defend its sovereignty and territorial integrity.

Excerpts from the interview;

Question: You are playing a key role in these extraordinary times to protect Ukraine's national interests; What challenges do you and your teammates face as a diplomat representing a country now at war with neighbouring Russia?

Answer: Our small in comparison but capable team in the Embassy is working hard to change the perception of Ukraine in the countries of our accreditation – India, Bangladesh Sri Lanka, Maldives, Nepal. It's a priority for Ukrainian Foreign Ministry, as it is stated by the President of Ukraine Volodymyr Zelenskyy, to work closer with the countries of Global South on different aspects of cooperation.

Q: Exactly one year ago, Russia launched a limited military action against your country calling it "demilitarisation and denazification". Please give a brief overview of the situation as this conflict has completed a year.

A: First of all let us please use the right words (terms) and timings. It's not just a conflict, and it's not a limited military action. It's Russian full scale war against Ukraine or Russian aggression against Ukraine. Russia is aggressor, Ukraine is a victim of Russian aggression.

In 2014 Russia started this war with illegal annexation of Crimea and further Russian aggression in the East of Ukraine. So we have 9 years of Russian war against Ukraine and 1 year of full scale aggression against Ukraine.

As of now Ukrainian Armed Forces could kick out Russian occupiers from 40% of territories occupied since February 2022. This spring will bring more victories on the battlefield for Ukraine.

Q: Some people are arguing that Ukraine is fighting someone else War; in fact, Ukraine is a "scapegoat", they say. May I have your take, please?

A: Ukrainians have never chosen war; it was imposed by Russia. This war is imperialist in its nature; one should understand this. Russia couldn't accept the collapse of Soviet Union and if they conquered Ukraine – that would be just a first step, they would continue this barbaric practices with other countries which they consider to be the sphere of their interests.

We are fighting for our freedom and independence. we fight

against Russia protecting others in Europe from this threat and our partners understand this very well.

Ukraine as any other democracy in the world wants to decide its destiny without external dictatorship which Russia tries to impose through our history.

We have our own will to join the EU and NATO as we consider ourselves as an integral part of Europe.

Q: At the beginning of the conflict, both countries tried to find a solution through negotiation. Do you still believe that Ukraine can find a solution through negotiation? If not, what is the way out?

A: Moscow has no intention for peace. When they talk about negotiations it means they want time to regroup and replenish supplies and further relaunch their attack on Ukraine. It's obvious.

Negotiations can happen and should happen one day. But the reason for the negotiations about future peace deal can only begin after unconditional withdrawal of Russian troops from the territory of Ukraine within the internationally recognised borders including Crimea. This is also stated in the UN General Assembly Resolution as of 23 February 2023, which was supported by 141 countries.

Q: What is the outcome of the 10 points peace formula introduced by your president but unfortunately, rejected by Russia stating that the formula is the basis for negotiations?

A: Russia has not yet shown any readiness to bring a lasting peace, and continues to perpetrate international terrorism, commit genocide against Ukrainians, and commit war crimes.

The Peace Formula's ten elements, which may be followed

collectively or individually, have the potential to bring about long-term peace in Ukraine, Europe, and the globe. We welcome countries from all across the world to join us in making it a reality.

The EU has approved President Zelenskyy's Peace Formula and committed to actively working with Ukraine to put it into action, which demonstrates that the Formula is completely consistent with core European values and ideals.

Ukrainian Peace Formula is based on respect for the sovereignty and territorial integrity of any country, with any aggression against a sovereign country being completely unacceptable and those responsible for any such acts facing justice.

Q: Do you think NATO and Western countries, who are pouring military equipment, will stand with Ukraine to find a lasting solution soon?

A: We are deeply grateful to all our allies and all peace-loving states of the world for their support in our fight against evil. Russia has to be defeated so this won't repeat in future. Our partners are clear – they will stand with Ukraine as long as it takes, till the victory. Victory of Ukraine is a victory of a democratic world.

Q: You are representing Ukraine in South Asia; tell us your take on the responses you have from the countries here.

A: The countries of our accreditation don't support Russia's aggression against Ukraine and this is very important. We are grateful for this position. I believe there is much more we can do to deepen our relationship on the mutually beneficial basis.

10

SRI LANKA DEBT CANCELLATION
RESPONSIBILITY OF GLOBAL SOUTH

The combination of colonial-era imperialism, debt crisis, political instability, and ethnic violence creates a toxic mix, resulting in unparalleled challenges.

~

Gary Dymski

Professor of Applied Economics at the Leeds University Business School in UK

SRI LANKA'S situation has to be widely publicized; there are other countries too – less prominent globally, smaller – who have unpayability problems, but none with the tortured contemporary history that your country is now living

It is time for the nations of the global South to build their own way, to self-organize, Gary Dymski, a well-known economist and Professor of Applied Economics at the Leeds University Business School in UK, said in an interview with me.

Who will lead them? Not Modi, nor Jinping. Who is the Kwame Nkrumah or Julius Nyerere or Sekou Toure of today;" he asked.

Gary Dymski is an excerpt on monetary economics; macroeconomic theory and policy; banking and financial institutions; economic development; political economy; urban economics; inequality; stratification economics. He has been a visiting scholar in universities and research centers in Australia, Brazil, Bangladesh, Colombia, Greece, India, Italy, Japan, Korea, and Mexico.

"Sri Lanka's situation has to be widely publicized; there are other countries too – less prominent globally, smaller – who have unpayability problems, but none with the tortured contemporary history that your country is now living," he observed.

"We need a repurposed set of development banks, controlled by progressive forces willing to move past the capitalist system. This does not yet exist," he suggested.

Being a member of the council of the Post Keynesian Economic Society (UK), Prof Dymski also is an advisor to the Debt and Development division of the United Nations Conference on Trade and Development (UNCTAD) in Geneva.

Excerpts of the interview;

Question: Are we passing through a period of the worse global recession that could lead to an unprecedented catastrophe? If yes, what is the way out?

Answer: We are in a global recession that could develop in an alarming way. There is already an emerging debt crisis that is catastrophic in many developing countries, and will likely get worse. The slowdown of economic activity as such is unlikely to degenerate into a collapse. But the stagnation will most likely continue. So it is more like strangulation of the economies of countries that are lower in the currency hierarchy. Businesses will fail; financing arrangements will either be sustained on a pretend-and-extend basis or will lead to default. India and China have somehow managed to sustain positive growth rates, but this is offset by the damage that Russia's Ukrainian war is doing to supply chains and agricultural exports.

Q: Collective action and collective responsibilities are two sides of the same coin which will help us to overcome present challenges. But, I wonder, how we can advocate for all countries to come together in a deeply polarized global society. Give us some food for thought, please.

A: Only when an acute crisis emerges, with the mechanisms for leading out of that crisis prove to be broken, will we see a global consensus for a new global framework toward cooperation emerge. The success of right-wing nationalist movements looking backward to conditions for economic reproduction that no longer exists is a huge barrier now; as those seeking softer ways forward look like naïve idealists, and those wanting to put up barriers to the outside world look like defenders of national honour.

The hope I can give you is this: we must see a renewal of impetus – the broad participation in – the 'global social forum' movement when it first began. A global generational mobilization, I think, which is pro-equality and pro-sustainability, critical of capitalism, and esp of financial globalization in the way its developed to now – feeding hyper inequality. I think it's possible. But this bottom-up, across-the-globe aspect has to be there, I think.

Q: You are one of the signatories who called for Sri Lanka debt cancellation. Do you think it is a realistic approach where all stakeholders shall come to a common platform to execute your demand?

A: The stakeholders have diverse interests; they must be forced to the table. Sri Lanka's situation has to be widely publicized; there are other countries too – less prominent globally, smaller – who have unpayability problems, but none with the tortured contemporary history that your country is now living. I think it has to be framed in terms of the 'harm and loss' debate that is now linking climate-change damage to legacies of colonialism and imperialism, not to mention the greater energy/non-renewable consumption of the elite global-North nations. This can be the basis of a common cause for debt forgiveness, I think. But the nations of the global South have to build their own way, to self-organize. Who will lead them? Not Modi, nor Jinping. Who is the Kwame Nkrumah or Julius Nyerere or Sekou Toure of today?

Q: Why do you think the case of Sri Lanka is essential to rethinking and reshaping the global economic order?

A: As answered earlier – the unique conjuncture of colonial-era imperialism, debt crisis, political instability and ethnic violence are a unique toxic mix, leading to unparalleled challenges.

Q: You have raised a vital point by alleging that International Financial Institutions of not living up to their responsibilities at a time when they are most urgently needed. Do we have an alternative?

A: There is no alternative now. We need a repurposed set of development banks, controlled by progressive forces willing to move past the capitalist system. This does not yet exist. The alternative can be imagined in a post-capitalist framework, in which nation-states are led by progressive leaders – enough of them – to force a global transfer mechanism for supporting the financing of the SDGs and climate sustainability on a world scale. I wish I had a different answer. For now, we must attempt to understand the scale of changes in systems of provision, supply chains, in localized production and consumption, required around the world.

The entities that have the capacity to support this are either too tied to capitalist priorities or they are not seeing the need to think holistically. It is not – it is never – too late. But we have to think beyond the limits that have prevented us from being strong enough to see the required planning framework clearly.

11

CHINA AND PAKISTAN ARE INDIA'S TWO MAJOR COMPETITORS

Pakistan remains politically sensitive, but is more an irritant than an existential challenge to New Delhi.

~

Dhruva Jaishankar
Executive Director of the ORF America

I THINK there were some integral design flaws in SAARC. In the 1980s because both India and Pakistan had concerns about the body being used to isolate them, it was agreed that it should operate by consensus.

"China and Pakistan are India's two major competitors with which it has major disputes over territory and other issues," Dhruva Jaishankar, Executive Director of the Observer Research Foundation America (ORF America) during our discussion. Jaishankar is a Non-Resident Fellow with the Lowy Institute in Australia and is a regular contributor to the media.

Jaishankar holds a bachelor's degree in history and classics from Macalester College, and a master's degree in security studies from Georgetown University. He has been an IISS-SAIS Merrill Center Young Strategist (2013), a participant in the ORF-Zeit Stiftung Asian Forum on Global Governance (2016), and a David Rockefeller Fellow with the Trilateral Commission (2017-2020).

Excerpts of the interview;

Question [A]: You are heading ORF America; what is your mission and what are the challenges you are facing in achieving your objectives?

Answer [A]: I joined the Observer Research Foundation in 2019 and moved to Washington DC with the intention of building up a think tank focused on policy for the United States, India, and their partner countries. I had worked previously in the U.S. at the Brookings Institution and German Marshall Fund, and in India at Brookings India (now the Centre for Social and Economic Progress), and had had affiliations with think tanks in Singapore and Australia, and hoped to build upon these experiences. I'm proud to say that in two plus years my colleagues and I have set up a small but dynamic U.S.-based institution, working on research and convening in four areas: international security, technology policy, energy and climate, and economic development. Our work is global in scope, including development in Africa, cyber security in Latin America, entrepreneurship in the Middle East, U.S.-India climate cooperation, and strategic cooperation involving the Quad and Europe, and we have a small but growing team of 10 staff. In some ways, ORF America occupies a useful niche, not just on U.S.-India relations but as the only developing world-affiliated public policy think tank in Washington.

Q: Who is India's main enemy in the context of foreign policy?

A: I don't think we're in a world defined by easy 'enemies' and India is not in a state of war with any country at the moment. However, India does have two major competitors with which it has major disputes over territory and other issues: China and Pakistan. In the past, the rivalry with Pakistan was predominant, involving Pakistani revisionism and its support for terrorism against India. However, in recent years, differences with China have become more acute, not just over the disputed border, but on trade and technology, regional politics, and a wide range of multilateral issues. Given that China's economy and capabilities are significantly greater than India's, it is fair to say that India's biggest strategic challenge today is China, not Pakistan. Pakistan remains politically sensitive, but is more an irritant than an existential challenge to New Delhi.

Q: India, not only, is supporting Quad but an active member. Simultaneously, India is keeping a strong relationship with Russia. However, many small countries in the same region argue that India continues to maintain its hegemony and does not allow those countries to take their own decisions; for example, Chinese investments. May I have your take, please?

A: Every country is sovereign and can make its own decisions, but the reality is that decisions made by neighbours do have political, economic, and security implications for each other. India has lots of natural alignments with the Quad on security and non-security issues, including over 20 active working groups. At the same time, India has important relations, particularly on defense trade and technology, with Russia. So it is natural for India to try to improve relations with the Quad partners, while preserving aspects of its relations with Moscow that are vital for national security and for its economy, such as energy costs and food security. Regarding the region, India has interests in a peaceful, stable, and prosperous South Asia, and has been taking steps to improve those relationships. These include greater diplomatic attention, improved connectivity, economic and technical assistance, and regionalism. At the same time, just as India has been sensitive to its neighbors concerns, it expects an understanding of issues that might implicate Indian politics, its economy, and its natural security. As a friend, it is important and healthy for India to voice concerns when decisions made by its neighbors might have negative spillover effects. Overall, India can always do more to treat its neighbors with respect and sensitivity, but that respect and sensitivity must be mutual.

Q: Compare to other regions in Asia, South Asian countries in particular is having lower socio-economic unity. Many argue that it is because of the rivalry between India and Pakistan. Because of that, organizations like SAARC have become paralyzed. Why can't these two nations come together for a serious development plan?

A: I think there were some integral design flaws in SAARC. In the 1980s because both India and Pakistan had concerns about the body being used to isolate them, it was agreed that it should operate by consensus. Yet on many issues – think for example about the proposed SAARC satellite – Pakistan blocked consensus. Pakistan also blocked connectivity between India and Afghanistan, including during the recent food crisis, before relenting. As a consequence, in recent years, there have been steps by India to operate regionally without relying on consensus. One example involves greater road connectivity between Nepal, India, and Bangladesh. Maritime coordination between India, Sri Lanka, and the Maldives has also improved. Barring Pakistan, there have been many positive developments on regional integration and connectivity: India and Nepal enjoy an open border and special relationship, India is among the largest investors and trade partners of Bangladesh, and India has led emergency lending to Sri Lanka. The questions of Pakistan must really be answered by Pakistanis: why has there been so much resistance to normal relations with India? The expectation that normal relations can coexist with state support for terrorists against Indian targets is unrealistic.

Q: Most Indian media houses have absolute anti-China stances. Isn't it toxic to the bilateral relationship between the two countries?

A: I'm not sure that's the case. The India-China relationship is mixed. Until quite recently there was cooperation on economic and trade issues, students, and on multilateral issues such as global governance reform and climate change. But under Xi Jinping, China has adopted a very different attitude to international affairs – and not just with India. As Chinese power has grown, its decision-making structures have become more opaque, it has engaged in non-market economic practices such as predatory lending, corporate espionage, and distortive subsidies, it has attempted territorial revisionism in the South China Sea and the disputed boundary with India, and it has made efforts to undermine many global norms and institutions, including on non-proliferation, outer space, and the law of the sea. These concerns are shared by many countries. With respect to India, we have seen China violate almost three decades of written agreements on border management, its dumping of exports while denying Indian companies market access, its undermining of India's regional security environment, and its blocking India at multilateral forums. Obviously, China deserves greater study and understanding, but some of the frustration reflected in Indian and international commentary reflects the recent actions and behavior of the Chinese government.

Q: Do you believe the Asian Century is an achievable reality?

A: It depends on what is meant by the Asian Century. It is quite clear that the future of global economic growth and international security will be decided in large part in Asia, simply because it is home to more than half the world's population and because of regional economic dynamism. But questions of whether Asia will be more cooperative or divisive will depend in large part on China's ability to respect other countries in its periphery. Unfortunately, that has been found wanting, and with slowing Chinese growth, other countries in the Indo-Pacific are naturally attempting to promote alternative values – freedom, openness, inclusivity – that should define an Asian Century.

Q: Do you think there will soon be a time when China, India and Russia will work together? If so, how do you formulate India's strategy?

A: China, India, and Russia do have some areas of commonality, and these have been explored in forums such as the RIC, BRICS, and Shanghai Cooperation Organization (SCO). Initially, this involved issues such as greater representation on forums of global governance and managing security in Central Asia. But the past few years have also shown limitations to such cooperation. Differences between China and India have been more acute, with China emerging as India's most significant strategic challenge. Russia's actions in Ukraine have presented some dilemmas to China and India. Barring security and some areas of strategic cooperation, the India-Russia agenda remains thin, largely on account of the limitations to the Russian economy. While we are likely to continue to see India engage with these forums, decisions made in Moscow and Beijing will ultimately determine how useful they will be.

12

OUR FOREIGN POLICY
FRIENDSHIP TO ALL; ENMITY TO NONE

The duty of a diplomat is not just to go out and give a flash statement to the audience and come back, but a lot of hard work underneath has to happen.

~

Ali Sabry
Minister of Foreign Affairs of Sri Lanka

WHAT is Sri Lanka's foreign policy and how Sri Lanka is pursuing its relationships with other countries during this most difficult period? I sat down with Ali Sabry PC, the Foreign Minister of Sri Lanka, to discuss various areas of the subject. In this lengthy interview, he offered his thoughts on opportunities and challenges ahead of Sri Lanka's moves to overcome prevailing challenges and become more global.

Excerpts from the interview;

Question: How do you define diplomacy and the role of a diplomat in Sri Lankan context?

Answer: Diplomacy is the most important area that defines our relationship with the outer world. It is kind of looking at the Sri Lankan perspective as well as regional and international viewpoints on how we become responsible international citizens, how we reach out to the outer world, how we protect our sovereignty while protecting and promoting Sri Lankan reputation and leveraging that notion to the nation's benefits, regional benefits, and ultimately the advancements of global peace and prosperity.

Q: We often called our foreign policy based on non-alignment but at the same time, it says our foreign policy is neutral. How can one become non-aligned at the same time being neutral?

A: Actually, we have been nonaligned, for a long period of time, but the Non-Aligned Movement (NAM), since the end of the cold war, where leading Asian politicians like Mrs Bandaranaike reaffirmed that we do not belong to this block and that block, is no longer active. Most of the members of the NAM have progressively become neutral. The principle that we are a neutral nation to the outer world is that we do not identify ourselves as part of any bloc against the greater good of humanity or global cooperation. That's why we have become neutral. Sometimes people blindly become neutral, but we don't do that.

In the meantime, despite being neutral in a practical world, we have our own interests, at the multilateral and regional levels on our trade, international-external security and so on. Therefore, from time to time we need to abide by some decisions in the light of our own national interests.

Everybody is doing the same thing. For us, our foreign policy is impetus by President Wickremesinghe, and as the Foreign Minister, myself the commitment is, to be Sri Lanka first. If you say anything else, it's not true. While being Sri Lanka first, how do we become a responsible international citizen and a regional player, instead of steering up tension, and how do we become a peacemaker? As a responsible and dignified member of the international community, our foreign policy is friendship to all, enmity to none.

Q: How can you help us to describe in one line if someone asked you what's our foreign policy?

A: Our foreign policy is neutral. While remaining neutral, we act in strategic Sri Lankan interests.

Q: In your recent speech, you say, that "the United Nations is a table where every State can sit down, a forum where everyone can be heard and where everyone is equally important." Is it a reality?

A: No, it is not a reality. What I tried to raise is that what we expect from multilateral platforms like the UN or other treaty bodies, is equal opportunity for all. But, in today's geopolitical division, and global north and south division, it is no longer happening. That's unfortunate. But, yet, we still don't have another alternative than pursuing the same multilateral forums and advocating for great reforms within. It is like Sri Lankan judicial system. People sometimes criticize. Just because of the criticisms, what will happen if you decided to take it away? There will be absolute anarchy then. Likewise, what is important is how to improve such a responsible global body while being a part of it. That's what we are promoting.

Q: Do you think that Global South is looking for an alternative?

A: There is a little bit of talk here and there. But I don't think a similar kind of movement like NAM from neutral bodies is any longer viable. Because big players are now aligned through different sectors and shapes, i.e. G7, BRICS, European Union, etc. These initiatives show that everybody is looking at their national interests. In a globalized world, national interests mean you continue to collaborate with the international community. That's where the opportunities lie, but at the same time, that's where the threats come from. Therefore, engagement is the most important principle in diplomacy. The first step is to continue engagement, as you can't put Iron Gate and tell that we are not going to talk with you anymore, though sometimes we felt disgraced. But we must continue to engage on all available platforms. Give our perspectives and get the best out of them.

Q: Earlier Sri Lanka's voice was heard and the opinions of policymakers and diplomats were matters in international forums. But now there is a sort of opinion saying that our voice is declining. Do you agree?

A: Comparatively, I would say, yes. But it has not been diminished, for example right now the First Committee of the UN which is involved in non-proliferation and disarmament is Chaired by a Sri Lankan. So we are influential and we are doing a lot of work there. And we are a much-respected member of the international community. In the region, we were the first country to open up but now that has changed and many countries have opened up. Almost everybody is into open trade and integrated with western markets. However, it is not that we have lost clout, but many countries emerged to contribute equally and sometimes even more.

Q: But, many people argue that unlike earlier, it is hard to see the substantive contributions from most of those who are working in Sri Lankan missions abroad. There are serious allegations over political appointees where many without a basic understanding of international affairs were installed in our missions. Isn't it impacting the country's reputation?

A: I think we need to get foreign experts in particular areas to head our mission. Well, there could be good inputs from outside, for example, some of our best diplomats were not from Foreign Service. If you take late Lakshman Kadirgamar who is the best Sri Lankan diplomat ever, he was not from Foreign Service. Likewise, we have to carefully pick and choose people to lead the mission not on political affinities or political leverage or our relationship with them but on merits. While we keep the Foreign Service as the backbone, Foreign Service alone cannot do this as we don't have the required number of officers. Therefore, we need those with integrity to get into serving us, as happened in the past. Well, I agree with you, we need to professionalize this, and we need to get politics out of it in a practical sense.

Having said that, I don't always agree with this unfair criticism against our diplomats. We just have 170 diplomats in over 60 missions to represent Sri Lanka in the whole world. We don't have resources compared with others. Like anything else we need to invest in diplomacy, we need to invest in their training. We have not recruited a batch of Foreign Service officers since 2018. If you look at the last fifteen years we have had just three batches of Foreign Service officers. So you can't do that and expect the best. We need to continue to recruit them, at least, once in two years. But, ideally, I would suggest, every year. That's why we need to look at alternative ways of getting our Sri Lankans who are well-settled in other countries, to get their service on voluntarily basis.

Q: Undoubtedly, you are doing a remarkable service, since you were appointed as the Minister of Foreign Affairs. But wonder if you can tell us more about how you evaluate the service of our missions abroad.

A: Basically, I addressed all of them via virtual platforms once in two months. Then I asked each desk responsible for each mission in the ministry to get detailed reports on the activities of every mission every two weeks. For the first time, I have introduced a bi-weekly meeting with the management of the Foreign Ministry, which means all additional secretaries to the ministry who are in charge of every mission and subject i.e. legal, trade, culture, etc. to sit with me and my state minister, to look at the progress.

The duty of a diplomat is not just to go out and give a flash statement to the audience and come back, but a lot of hard work underneath has to happen. Unless everybody works in the same direction, same passion, and with the same vision achieving objectives is difficult. We have slowly put those principles into practice.

Yes, we need a few resources too, for example, in the whole public diplomacy division in the ministry we just have one Foreign Service officer. We don't have people to deploy there. The whole legal division has just four lawyers whereas about 200 treaties are pending. These are huge challenges. We need to carefully look at this and upgrade it.

You would have seen when I was in Justice Ministry; a lot of reforms taking place. Likewise, some people might think Foreign Minister or a diplomat somewhere can go and do wonders and come. No, it is not like that. It is a reflection of the local policies. Local policies are important. Everything that is happening here goes public the moment it happened as we are not a closed country. Therefore, first, we need to achieve progress domestically in the required areas such as accountability, constitutionalism, power devolution, advancements in human rights protection, childcare, education, etc. before we blame a few of our diplomats abroad. Then we can go and represent somewhere else. Our domestic achievements are reflected in our diplomacy. Even to do that we need to have an organized structure. If that structure is not strong enough, it is very difficult for us to deliver.

Q: You meant to say the prevailing structure is weak?

A: Yes, extremely weak.

Q: What are the reasons behind this weakness?

A: We have not holistically looked into the system for a long period of time. The ministry has several limbs, it is not only about the faces talking at the UN and elsewhere but a lot of hard work involved. How strong our UN division, research division, how strong our West desk and South Asian Desk are, as well as other related institutes are very important. It is reflected in our foreign policy. What an individual can do is decorate the cake but the cake has to be baked properly with good ingredients.

Q: Do you have a strategy to revamp the system?

A: Yes, even in the midst of economic challenges, we are making it work. I can't go to the phase which I would love to go, in terms of recruitment and so on. But definitely, we are working on it.

Q: Let's talk about regional affairs, what is your opinion about SAARC?

A: In fact, SAARC has not achieved expected objectives fully though it was formed a long time ago. If you compared it with the ASEAN, they have gained a lot. Unfortunately, members within the SAARC are not united in their vision and mission. Hence it has hindered SAARC from real progress. I think, either we need to revamp the SAARC and have a very frank and open discussion about its progress or we may have to look beyond the SAARC.

Q: I assume the same thought you will have about the Colombo Plan as well?

A: Yes. It is time to look for other pragmatic organizations. Even BIMSTEC had not given the expected returns. Probably, IORA, Japan and China-based Think Tanks and related initiatives, will be good places for us to be concerned. President Wickremesinghe is also concerned about the progress of regional bodies like SAARC. I know we need to look at them carefully, but so far it's been a great disappointment, to say the least.

Q: As you say, ASEAN is one of the most efficacious regional bodies. Sri Lanka tried to get membership since the beginning but is yet to succeed. Why?

A: I think probably the location per se if you see all members who are clubbed together in ASEAN. We are far away from them. However, we are an observer state, and we need to see how we can operate as ASEAN is a remarkable success in terms of tariff in trade, investments, and other bilateral and multilateral affairs. But, we have not achieved expectations, though we have opened our market at a very early stage.

Unfortunately, we have gone back to protectionism. Protectionism is not the right way to do as the end of the day it will eliminate your productivity and ability for innovation, and you will never become an export-oriented country if you are going down with the protectionist past. That's what exactly happened here. Sri Lanka has 31% of exports in the early 90s but now it has decreased to 15%, that's because we don't protect the local manufacturers to serve the Sri Lankan market and they are not competitive enough in the international market. Consequently, their products cannot sale outside. That is the simple formula. Luckily, tourism was gained, and the war ended though we did not realize the huge benefit of them. But then tourism came to end and we faced different social scenarios where our remittent drastically came down, then the reality called. That is what exactly we are facing today. The long-term strategy or long-term prosperity of Sri Lanka is dependent upon the economy which is based on sustainable exports.

Q: Right now we are facing the worst economic crisis since our independence. Do you recognize this as a national calamity?

A: Yes, of course. This is the biggest economic calamity this country has ever experienced. It is the result of a combination of reasons including bad debt inherited for a long period and bad luck due to the Easter Sunday Attack, Covid-19, and the War in Ukraine which caused international instability as well as bad monetary, bad agrarian and bad cultural policies which antagonized particularly the Muslim countries. So it is a combination of debt inheritance, bad luck, and bad policies that brought us here where we are today. We are in a very difficult time. Not only we, but we probably are the first but more than 50 countries are on the lope due to Covid-19 and subsequent international disorder in view of the Ukrainian crisis.

Q: But, what prevented you from taking precautions, especially at a time when a person like you who has an in-depth understanding of contemporary issues, was playing an active role?

A: Unfortunately, what has happened is the economy was handled by a few people. It was never debated in detail at the cabinet. Most critical decisions were taken by a handful of officials. And they were not willing to listen. True, we were not economists per se but we had good readings and constructive discussions and went to the cabinet and suggested we must go to IMF, we must slowly depreciate the local currency to encourage the inflow of remittance which will avoid the "undial", "hawala" or any other illegal practices. Not me but most of the cabinet colleagues were telling that the decision to go total organic fertilizer is not good, but then those voices were not heard and respected. Those are the problem we faced, and I fought very hard to reverse that forced cremation which has clearly antagonized the entire Muslim community here and abroad. These are all unnecessary things that have happened and we should learn from them. Sometimes you felt helpless, though you have views no one is listening to though you get time to put them, especially, when you are not in a decision-making position.

However, during my time as the Minister of Justice, I was given free hand and I did a lot of work. That's how I was able to increase the number of courts, appointments, recruitments, and clear backlogs. We have drafted around 10 new laws. We were taking a holistic approach to reengineering the existing system in the justice ministry. But in the economy, we were not the decision-makers. When not only mine but genuine experts' opinions are being disregarded, then what can you do? They should have listened to them.

Q: Right, do you think at the moment, that policymakers have diagnosed our real problem?

A: Right now, one good thing is that we are now engaging with the world's best institutes like IMF, World Bank, ADB, UNDP, etc., and taking steps to reshape our economy. When I was appointed as the Finance Minister, in a very short period of time, we took a firm decision including approaching the IMF and World Bank, Suspending the debt to ensure the right to livelihood of every citizen, hiring the world's best to get support to normalize the situation. Luckily, President Wickremesinghe's economic literacy is very high compared to any other leader. He knows that. And now he is leading the subject. I think we have diagnosed the problem properly. But it requires long-term medication. Stability is entirely depending on how we are going to continue this medication or if we are abandoning it halfway through. If we can do that like how India did in 1991, we will have a future; otherwise, our future is bleak.

Q: So what is your gut feeling saying?

A: It all depends on how our leaders are taking action. I have a lot of confidence in the President but others need to follow and support him. And the opposition too must realize and understand not to play politics with Sri Lanka's economy. India did it from 1991 to 2023. India opened its economy in 1991. Dr Manmohan Sing being the Finance Minister introduced the reforms. Every political party irrespective of huge differences in their political viewpoints supported and continued those policies. They are reaping the benefits today. They will become the third economy by 2029. That is because of the consistency of the policies based on national interests.

There has to be an unwritten yet conscientious agreement among all politicians and the parties here, we will all do our politics, and we will have our policy differences and all but there are two areas we should not get involved. First education, we must continue to invest in education, and give English and IT-based education. The second economy, economic policy must be pursued consistently by inviting and permitting foreign investments. Relying only on foreign remittance and tourism is dangerous as they are extremely vulnerable. Look at China's case, and India's case, even in Bangladesh when the whole world was closed their economies were growing. They are suppliers, but we are not. Their economy is based on a broadly strategically designed export orientation. Therefore, they are not vulnerable as us. We can open the country but no one is coming in because social scenarios, such as terror attacks and the pandemic, took us down. That is why we can't solely rely on dynamic areas like tourism or foreign remittent. This is the time we must do the required changes in our economy.

Q: Let me, once again, pay attention to your recent speech at the UN where you quoted President Wickremesinghe about social reforms, "I will implement social and political reforms requested by the nation". Same time, a few media in the city have reported that Sri Lanka is going to establish a South African model truth and reconciliation commission. May I have your take, please?

A: That is one of the most important areas. Since the end of the war, we must accept that real reconciliation between the North and the South has not been undertaken. True, the war ended, and we have gained "peace" but real reconciliation has not taken place. We need to put effort into it. Because we have not done so, we are giving undue advantage to the enemy who's against Sri Lanka all over the world saying that you have spoken about it but you have not done anything substantive. That's very unfair because Sri Lankan forces, as a whole, did a tremendous job to restore peace and social order in this country. The benefits of that are for all Sri Lankans, particularly for Tamil people who were suffering the most because that was the theatre of the war.

But pointing finger at the forces and naming them as perpetrators of human rights abuses is very unfair. They also need a platform to redeem themselves. And if somebody or a few of them had done something excessive they should also be looked into and prosecuted. We must prove that we are capable of doing that as a country. If we don't do that, then we are keeping the case open for foreigners to come and meddle. The first step was already taken by the UN Human Rights Council by establishing an external evidence-gathering mechanism. If it goes to the next level, they will go and start to investigate Sri Lanka at various forums. In order to not only prevent that but also actually reach a true reconciliation through our undertaking is that we are coming out with the domestic mechanism.

It will help us to protect our overall military establishment. If you are concerned about all these issues, we owe a duty to the country to establish our own truth and reconciliation mechanism like in South Africa. Once and for all people can come and talk about it and move away from the very dark past. So we learn from it, in order to not to commit it again to do the same mistakes that we have committed.

Q: How can you establish public trust in order to move forward with this, as you know whenever we talk about this subject, certain segments of society will come up and tell that this is a great plot against the armed forces and a few others?

A: That's important. But we need to have a mechanism to talk to different people and get a wider consensus as much as possible. Actually, we need to establish this to prevent the armed forces from being prosecuted outside. That's precisely the case. Well, if you don't do it, that danger is looming and it will become even closer. Already our top commanders cannot travel, some others have been closely looked at and their family members have been flatted. It is unfair for what they have done for this country. Some of the divisions in the army, which are the best divisions we have, all together have been blacklisted from UN peacekeeping. In order to get rid of it also, it is important to implement this mechanism.

Another point I must emphasize is that some people give the impression to the outside world that Sri Lankan forces have committed Genocide. However, I saw some of them mostly Tamils abroad come on my social media handle and say that they want to contribute to real reconciliation as they feel that they owe to this country. They say that they are here today because of free education, free health, and other social welfare facilities in Sri Lanka at the time. But, certain groups are propagating that Genocide has been committed in Sri Lanka. That's a blatant lie. We need a platform to show that there was no Genocide here. True, it was a dark conflict. When someone came and say this, I asked them, do you know how many Sri Lankan forces were killed; they don't have any clue about it. Then I told them, more than 26000 Sri Lankan forces and around 1200 Indian forces were killed. That was a fight against terrorism. Of course, there were casualties, representing every ethnic group. We need to get this clear picture out. How can we do that? Well, through this kind of mechanism. It is not easy; it will be opening up a can of worms. But, there is no other alternative. The idea is not retributive punishment of people. It is a kind of reconciliation, truth-seeking, reparation-based mechanism. Only extreme cases of clear violations of human rights abuses need to be prosecuted. This is not a Nuremberg that we are talking about; this is a kind of South African model, a truth-seeking mechanism.

Q: At the same time, there were talks about the devolution of power. Our neighbouring country, India, is suggesting to us full implementation of 13th Amendment to the constitution. Do you think it will solve our problem?

A: I think the parliamentary subcommittee should carefully look at devolution. Having come a long way on the 13th Amendment, we can't now reverse it either. But there are areas of concern such as to which extent police power and land power we can give. Subject to that, governing by the people of the area is not a bad idea. They have most interests in their lands, subject to safeguards of the sovereignty and territorial integrity of the country.

Q: But what about the idea such as re-merging North and East?

A: No. The Supreme Court itself has ruled out and de-merged it. I don't think we should revisit that. Basically, let the North run on its own and let the East run on its own with respect to demography till we build trust between each other where ethnicity or religious beliefs are no longer the subjects but a meritocracy. There will be a day but till then we will have to find the best way we could to live together and move forward.

Still, there is a campaign for a separate state. As long as that threat remains, very difficult for us to disregard the tendency for secession as 99% of Sri Lankans are not even in their wildest dream thinking of a Separate State.

Q: Do you think co-sponsoring the UN Resolution on Sir Lanka was a fatal mistake by the previous administration?

A: I would not go back and find what was right or wrong. That was a different strategy, probably, at that time to overcome the challenges. But, we cannot do it because it goes against our constitution. As per the constitution, even if you want, foreign judges or hybrid judges are not allowed. That's the separate arm of the constitution. They have been appointed by the judicial commission; even the President cannot do it. That's precisely why having to cosponsor the resolution 2015; in 2019 our Foreign Minister who was a former Attorney General went to Geneva and explained this legal ramification. I think people understood that. Now, when I explained to the President, he also understood that. That is why after deliberating all options, we took this decision, the stance, which we have taken this time. We say that we will not allow you to meddle with our constitution. Internal matters are to Sri Lanka. But Sri Lanka will provide a total mechanism and we are serious about that.

Q: There were some thoughts spreading around that our relationship with India is weakening due to the Chinese presence here. Is that true?

A: Not really. We are continuing to strengthen our bilateral relationship at every level. Of course, challenges are there, like any other relationship, over each other's perceptions on certain issues. As Sri Lankans we need all of them, we need regional powers. Indian security is important to us. We can't have a stormy situation in our backyard.

In the same meantime, China is also our long-term friend. They have maintained a steady relationship with Sri Lanka as well as with the international community. China is the biggest investor in the country. We can't ignore it. We must find a way to work with all.

Q: Many people are talking about Chinese Debt Trap diplomacy. Do you agree?

A: No, I don't agree with it. That's a Sinophobic statement. China came here for investments, much-needed investments for Sri Lanka. For example, Hambantota Port was open to anyone, but the Chinese were shown the opportunity to put in their money and got it. Then Shangri-La that too was offered to everyone but the Chinese came and they invested in it. Colombo Port City is also the same. They are investors, and they take risks by investing in these massive investments.

When it comes to debt, they have not come and offered us debt but we have gone and asked them. We borrowed them voluntarily. I meant nothing wrong in borrowing debt as long as it is properly utilized for the purpose. And you pay back accordingly. It's not China's problem but our problem. Having borrowed the money, whether we have used it smartly or invested smartly, in a manner which gives you return so then you can pay back. If you haven't done that it is your problem. This is like going to the bank to get a loan to build a house and instead of building a house; you buy a car and blame the bank.

We are not here to encourage Sinophobia, that's why our foreign policy is neutral. We don't want to take a side; our relationship is based on merits. We need India, the West and China and everyone else. All of them are equally important to us. China is the biggest investor, the West is the biggest market for us, and India is our neighbour who has stood for us during this extremely difficult time. And we managed to end the armed conflict due to India's firm stance. Destabilizing these relationships is suicidal for Sri Lanka. The bottom line is everyone is important to us.

This is a complicated situation. But we are doing our level best. Sincerely, engaging with them, and talking to them frankly without duping them or giving them false speeches is our way. The policy we are pursuing is honest with all our external relationships.

Q: But, if you take the recent events, such as detaining of the Russian passenger flight and the controversy over docking Yuan Wang 5 Research vessel, telling us otherwise. Don'tthey?

A: I think the Russian passenger flight (Aeroflot) situation is totally different where Sri Lankan government has not had any hand in that. That was an order given by the court. But later we looked into the matter, and Attorney General made the submission. Then the matter was sorted out.

But, yes, Yuan Wang 5 is a different scenario. There were so many not only research but many military vessels docking at our ports that nobody has raised any concern. But this particular Vessel is different. Unfortunately, clearance had been given during the political turmoil, where most institutes were in dilemma. But, when someone comes and says that this is a threat, it is our duty to ask for evidence. If there is evidence, then we could have acted otherwise. In absence of evidence, it is not fair for us to recall permission which has already been given. Chinese are our friends and we requested them to pause it for some time until we relooked at it. Then we called our other friend to share the information. There was nothing that warranted for us to overturn the original decision of clearance. We decided to go ahead.

Q: The third incident in a similar shape is the controversy over the Chinese fertilizer ship.

A: It is nothing to do with diplomacy but a commercial transaction. But it is indeed complex. If you look at the company that bought the shipment, that is one of the biggest companies in the world that provide organic fertilizer. They will not tarnish their image for a small shipment like this. They have got clearance from Singapore and Switzerland, who have the best laboratories in the world, but not from Sri Lanka. I don't know what exactly went behind this.

Sometimes it is not as simple as you see it. There can be sabotage taking place at individual interests. It is a great loss to the country and a great loss to our future just like what has happened because of the forced cremation. So-called self-proclaimed geoscientists and a few others went against the whole world and the country was forced to follow which resulted in greater isolation of Sri Lanka. That was just because they maintained a kind of hate against a particular community in Sri Lanka. Their hate overtakes the rationale and national interests of the country. These are the incidents I'm really worried about and every Sri Lankan has a responsibility to see the holistic picture to be rational and strategic despite treating your ambitions. A decision has to be merit-based.

Q: For the first time in history, the UK is having an Indian-origin man as their Prime Minister. The UK Parliament is scheduled to have a debate on Sri Lanka's human rights situation on November 9, in three days. What is your message to the Prime Minister and the debate that they are going to have on Sri Lanka?

A: We need to continually engage with the United Kingdom, as well as with other countries. We need to understand that both UK and Canada have a strong Sri Lankan Diaspora which can change the outcome of the votes in several electorates. That put a lot of pressure on the people who are being elected from those seats. That's the ground reality. They may use it, and we need to give our side of the story. But, to get over the allegations against us, we also have to perform domestically. What they have been telling us for a long period is accountability. If you provide a truth-seeking mechanism and accountability mechanism domestically, then we will have something to go and present by saying 'don't come and interfere in this because we are doing it.' Beyond that, we can't do anything. These threats are there, particularly in UK and Canada because of their voting power.

Sri Lanka's relationship with the UK is longstanding. We have a lot of similarities between us. Instead of a few isolated incidents-based complaints, we are requesting the new Prime Minister to look at the larger picture of Sri Lankan democracy. An elected President is forced to give up and go halfway through. Sri Lanka has thrived in democracy since 1931. Our elections are free and fair. None of the government leaders stays beyond their mandate. Let's work together. My message is very clear, let us work as partners and do not be misled by a few people with ulterior motives and hidden agendas for their political gain. Support Sri Lanka to recover fast.

Q: In conclusion, please offer us your thought on President's idea to establish the "Diaspora Office." How are you going to attract Sri Lankan expatriates for greater contributions to do better for the country through this initiative?

A: The idea is to connect all Sri Lankans overseas and foreigners of Sri Lankan origins. We will have a separate office here and we will connect them all through our missions abroad where we will provide our services including proper guidance to channel their investments in Sri Lanka. We are in the final process of designing it. Hopefully, we will be able to launch this initiative on the upcoming Independence Day.

13

HOW WE REFORM INDIAN ECONOMY

Reforms have to be thought out in all its dimensions of their short, medium and long term impact on a nation's people and also its external ramifications.

~

M. Sivaraman Ramanathan
Former Revenue Secretary, India

RENOWNED for his pivotal role in reshaping the landscape of excise and customs duties in India, M R Sivaraman emerges as a transformative figure who left an indelible mark on the nation's fiscal policies. As the former Revenue Secretary, Sivaraman's strategic vision and insightful leadership played a crucial role in overhauling the structure of excise and customs duties. His bold initiatives and innovative reforms have not only streamlined the taxation system but also paved the way for a more transparent and efficient revenue collection process.

"Dr. Singh allowed me to formulate all taxation reforms and I worked them out with some brilliant officers of the Indian Revenue Service," he recalled when I asked about the secrets behind the success in solving one of the most difficult economic crises India ever encountered. In his mid-twenties, he was the youngest collector ever in India and his journey is a very important trail to understanding what India is today. Revenue Secretary M R Sivaraman, who transformed the structure of excise and customs duties in India, shared his experiences not only on his personal journey but also on the institutions he worked for, including the International Monetary Fund.

Joining the I.A.S. cadre of Madhya Pradesh in 1962 Mr. M. Sivaraman Ramanathan has worked in various departments in the state of Madhya Pradesh and the Central Government. With over 40 years of experience, he has held important positions at various levels in the Department of Finance, Planning, Finance Commission, Economic Affairs and Ministry of Commerce and Finance. He has worked as Director-General of Civil Aviation & Ex-Officio Additional Secretary of Government of India, Ministry of Civil Aviation & Revenue Secretary, Government of India, Ministry of Finance, New Delhi. He has also worked as Executive Director, International Monetary Fund and was an Expert Adviser to the UN Security Council Committee to Counter-Terrorism. Currently he is engaged in delivering lectures on Budget, Banking, Fiscal and Monetary policies. While talking about the crisis in Sri Lanka he says, "Sri Lanka should not be attracted toward models of other countries. There is a temptation that the Chinese model is great or the American model is superb. These countries do not offer assistance for charity and they have their own agenda." Acclaimed author on fiscal and monetary policy issues Mr. Sivaraman reaffirmed that, "dynasty rule should be avoided at all costs," while identifying the foundation for a regime that sincerely respects liberty, equality, fraternity without hesitating to admit India's mistakes in the past in dealing with certain issues in Sri Lanka.

Excerpts of the interview;

Question: Mr Sivaraman, as a Chinese saying goes, we are living in an interesting time. Aren't we? The unpredictability of social calamities is becoming the norm. I, most of the time, was surprised to realize the gravity of the old Hegelian saying later popularized by Marx, "history repeats itself, first as tragedy, second as farce." Let's start this discussion on your early years as a dynamic youth. Born in British India in the 1940s and became the youngest collector ever in India at the age of 25, your footprints are a trail of what India today, as one of the main economies on the planet. Let's recall your early professional experiences and challenges such as corruption and bribery you saw, and how do you overcome them?

A: My first encounter with corruption was when as an assistant collector I was asked to trap a corrupt forest range officer.

The man who was asked for the bribe carried marked currency notes to the RO in a remote forest guest house and I was (all of 23 years) was waiting behind a tree near the guest house at around midnight. As soon as the notes were handed over to the RO I pounced on him with a few cops and arrested him. He tried to set his dog on us but it was caught. Then when I was collector I had caught red -handed, a senior Government of India official with a hefty bribe in his hands. Corruption is endemic in every society in different forms. There is also moral corruption when you see something going wrong and you do not stop it for fear of personal consequences. This is the worst form. In my 39 years service I was never afraid of speaking the truth almost following the Kantian categorical imperative excepting when I had to deal with my country's safety. I had not tolerated corruption in my vast revenue department as its permanent secretary and sent a few to jail and a few I dismissed from service using a rarely used constitutional provision and my orders were upheld by the courts also.

Q: India faces several financial downturns. One of the known scenarios was during the late Prime Minister P.V. Narasimha Rao's tenure. Political instability was on a rampage, social insecurity is at the helm and the forex balance was shaking. But, Rao's political wisdom changed the fate of the nation. He took the firmed decisions to restructure the Indian system to benefit all walks of the society. Everybody knows, that his handpick Dr Manmhohan Singh was the man behind this remarkable achievement. However, it is a smokescreen that an individual thinks that he/she alone can succeed in complicated social issues without the genuine support of a reliable and efficient team. You were the Revenue Secretary of India when Dr Singh was the Finance Minister. I know you have discussed the secrets behind this success story in many national and international forums. But I would like to have glimpses of your role and memorable incidents that you could like to recall today?

A: I had known Dr. Manmohan Singh since 1977 when I joined the Department of Economic Affairs as Director and he was my Secretary. Later he was instrumental in my getting posted as Joint Secretary there giving me opportunities to lead many intergovernmental talks and also accompany the PM on her state visits. Dr. Singh allowed me to formulate all taxation reforms and I worked them out with some brilliant officers of the Indian Revenue Service. Never did he reject any proposal of mine in the 4.5 years we were together. On one occasion I had a serious difference of opinion with him in the matter of relieving from the post of chairman of a Tribunal (equal to a High Court Judge in India) I relieved him using my position as administrative head of the Department and Dr. Singh was under political pressure to continue him not because he considered him worthy but the pressure was intense including from the PM. I declined and offered to proceed on leave. He then took the papers, studied them and agreed with me and told the PM that he would not like to overrule me. The PM P V Narasimha Rao did not overrule me. Dr. Singh was gentle and humane and kept a clean conscience as Finance Minister.

Several political luminaries including senior Cabinet Ministers came under a cloud with the SC monitoring a case of corruption under investigation by my department. Never ever I was asked to do anything contrary to my conscience and some of the cases involving surviving politicians are still pending in the court.

In my 36 years of service in the IAS never had I done anything against my conscience and nobody ever asked me to do anything. Mr. Arjun Singh the CM of MP had to quit because of a court judgement that upheld my view as correct opposing a cabinet decision. Even opposition party chiefs were always happy with the actions being taken by me. On a few occasions there were differences of opinion between me and Montek Singh Ahluwalia Secretary Economic Affairs but invariably Dr. Singh went along with me and so did Ahluwalia.

When I approved action against Sasikala the friend of Jayalalitha then CM of Tamil Nadu there was uproar in TN and a few people committed suicide. The PM who had the support of Jayalalitha did not stop me. Was it sheer luck or a considered decision by the PM and the FM to stand by me in my tough actions so that the people of India would know that the govt. will allow rule of law to take its course.

I would not know. But this puts the two political leaders on a pedestal at least during my time. Consistency in such an approach makes a person a great leader. But many fall on the wayside, unable to resist pressures or suffer personal consequences.

Q: You have redesigned and reengineered the function of the Central Excise and Customs of India. Why did you think it was such an essential area that needed to be addressed immediately?

A: The Customs and Central Excise department was characterised by corruption and the only way to reduce it was by making it rule based by removing discretion and all other changes in the tax system were toward that end. When for the first time the Delhi customs was to go online in a new building the construction of which I had supervised the then current Chairman would not come for its inauguration by Dr. Singh when four other former chairmen were present. He thought that it was my project an IAS officer's and so he should boycott it. While all the 4 former chairmen lauded the effort this gentleman was absent. He was fired by Dr. Singh later when he refused to attend to even budget files. The Custom House Agents tried to sabotage the system with the assistance of subordinate customs officials whose outside incomes disappeared. But we did not budge. Similarly computers were introduced in the management of Central Excise also.

The Permanent Account Number (PAN) was introduced during my time and now it is ubiquitous in India, a dream of mine that has been realised. It is also the basis of the registration for the GST also which I had suggested when the PAN became a reality. This wholesale computerisation removed discretion at the hands of officers and drastically reduced corruption, speeded up procedures facilitating commerce and business and reduced transaction costs. Dr. Singh supported every one of these decisions. Today India's taxation system is computerised from end to end thanks to the initial unfailing support by Dr. Singh and also the PM. Today's GST Council of India has its origin in the first State Finance Minister's conference organised under Dr. Singh to consider the introduction of the VAT in all the astes.

Q: Before we are going talk about your experiences at IMF, let me ask you about an existing socio-political issue on political leadership in South Asia and elsewhere. As Plato quoted Socrates, "no man chooses evil because it is evil; he only mistakes it for happiness". I find this statement is remarkably true, not only in ancient Greek but its validity holds even in most of the social affairs today. Mr Sivaraman, Why do leaders fail, though they tried their best to revamp the rotten system?

A: Reforms have to be thought out in all its dimensions of their short, medium and long term impact on a nation's people and also its external ramifications. When a government has formulated reforms with those considerations in view Leaders who do not devote their heart and soul in implementing those reforms and who are morally imperfect fail. This is true also of Bureaucrats who implement reforms and Political leaders who defend them in public and parliament. A leader must have a high moral calibre that he/she is incorruptible, courageous enough to sacrifice, put public welfare above self and be above suspicion. In today's world you have to search to find one unfortunately.

Q: After successful years in Indian Administrative Service, your next hold was in International Monetary Fund (IMF). What triggered you to join the IMF? Who are the remarkable economists you worked with?

A: Mr. P C Chidambaram a brilliant lawyer every inch an aristocrat succeeded DR. Singh as the Finance Minister but from a different regional political party of TN having resigned from the Congress.

I had a very good equation with him and we put through one budget together.

I never looked for any major assignment as I was certain that I had no political back up. But surprisingly Chidambaram called me in June 1996 and asked me why I had not approached him for a posting in the IMF or the Word Bank as ED, both the posts being vacant. I told him I was not aware of those vacancies. So I also offered to be considered. But after a few hours Mr. Chidambaram called me and said the PM Deve Gowda and some members of the cabinet wanted me to be the next Cabinet Secretary. I was taken aback as there were a few seniors in the service. Chidambaram told me that the seniors have been considered and were rejected and two of them could be appointed to the IMF and the WB. I told him I would accept whatever the government offered me. But political pressure mounted on the PM for Cabinet Secretary's post as well as for the others. Finally, the PM called me and said that he was making TSR Subramanian a 1961 batch officer and senior-most, although with only 3 months service left as the Cabinet Secretary. He was a fine officer and richly deserved the post. So I had to choose between the World Bank and the IMF.

Montek Ahluwalia a fair man told Chidambaram that I should be sent to the IMF as there one had to actively participate in policy making and will be confronted with the views of some of the world's leading economists and Surendra Singh the outgoing Cabinet Secretary not an expert in financial management who had been promised one of the posts by PM P. V. Narasimha Rao should be sent to the World Bank. That is how I got posted to the IMF.

Q: When you listen to many talks in day to day discussion it's clear that many people do not know much about what IMF is and its structural functionality. Correct me if I am wrong, IMF is not a charity but another bank with enormous commitments and different capabilities compared to our local banks. It borrows money from various nations to make it work and lends guarantees or other financial packages to countries in need. So my question is what are the basic principles you need to keep in mind when you approach the IMF for relief?

A: The IMF is an institution which basically tries to maintain the International Monetary System and exchange rates stable, for an orderly conduct of global trade and prevent crises in one country affecting other countries. That is why the Fund has Article IV consultations with member countries built into its charter. In most cases it is an annual exercise and in some it may have different periodicity also. These consultations enable the Fund to evaluate a country's policies from global a perspective as well from its national objectives. Its advice is not mandatory supplies but the Fund cautions a country when it sees dangers ahead.

When one approaches the IMF for assistance a country has to be sure that they may have to renounce populist decisions and adopt policies that initially may be unpalatable like pricing power and other forms of energy supplies like petrol and diesel at economic cost. Reform sales and income taxation to ensure that they are collected properly. To take measures to promote exports by having realistic exchange rate and monetary policies. On the fiscal front governments have to give up profligate policies. IMF these days are careful to ensure that their conditionalities do not affect the poor. Governments can negotiate conditionalities with the IMF.

Q: Do you think IMF is the panacea for the economic downturn? What are the success stories of IMF?

A: The IMF is not a panacea for all crises. IMF succeeded in the SEA crises by arresting the exit of international banks from the affected countries even though critics condemned many conditionalities of the IMF. I was there and some measures I had opposed myself. The IMF realised its mistakes as can be seen in the evaluation report on its performance during the crisis.

Q: Among other accounts, I was engrossed by a critical analysis of IMF and World Bank where the authors suggested these organizations are turning poor countries into loans addicted countries. I quote, "Once countries accepted the conditions of structural adjustment, the World Bank and the IMF rewarded them with still more loans, thus deepening their indebtedness—rather like a fireman pouring gasoline on a burning house to stop the blaze." What do you think? Is there an example you would like to tell that the IMF could have done better than they did?

A: Some criticisms of the IMF are valid as the economists there are mostly theoreticians and have had very little practical experience in handling crises of any country. There are very few, probably none in the IMF who has been a Finance Secretary of a country handling such a crisis. Mere theoretical solutions to every crisis do not work as economics is not an exact science.

Q: Mr Sivaraman, let's talk about Sri Lanka. I'm sure you need no foreword about the situation in Sri Lanka. You are one of the few who have in-depth knowledge reference to economic condition in this beautiful Island nation, your immediate neighbor. How do you read the situation, and what went wrong here in Sri Lanka?

A: I had the honour of representing Sri Lanka in the IMF. It is a beautiful country which successfully controlled its population, achieved near universal literacy, promoted health of every citizen and was attracting the attention of tourists and also administrators elsewhere on its success in achieving a satisfied society.

But political struggles amongst various groups became intense after the elimination of the LTTE. Actually, the return of peace should have catapulted the country to higher growth. This did not happen as the country could not resolve the Tamil issue. The hatred for Tamils by the Sinhalese and vice versa if not eliminated Sri Lanka will never be able to achieve its full potential. Both Tamil leaders and other leaders in Sri Lanka have to adopt a policy of give and take. Tamils must think as Sri Lankans and Sinhalese too have to cease being Sinhalese and be Sri Lankans. They cannot fight as they say like kilkenny cats as then only two tails will be left.

Q: You and one of the known intellects with whom I was fortune to keep fruitful communications for decades, Dr V Suryanarayan from the University of Madras, recently wrote an article about the Sri Lankan situation. The article ended by quoting the famous lines of Shakespeare in Macbeth echoes in our minds: "Alas, poor country, almost afraid to know itself. It cannot be called our mother, but our grave ..." This, I believe, is an attempt to get the worse scenario correct. What is the way out? Apart from giving priority to monkey politics, how can the country's resources be mobilized to overcome this tragic situation?

A: Sri Lanka should not be attracted toward models of other countries. There is a temptation that the Chinese model is great or the American model is superb. These countries do not offer assistance for charity and they have their own agenda. Similarly putting one country against another is a game that should be avoided. You may ask what about India. Yes India has its own interests to protect like it does not want to have countries hostile to it having bases economic or military in its neighbourhood.

I know India's record dealing with the LTTE has not been correct to say the least. But neither India nor Sri Lanka can forget that they are linked for over 2000 years culturally and historically. History may contain many mistakes but they have to be forgotten and move on for a better future.

India has a moral responsibility to ensure peace and stability in Sri Lanka so that its people live in peace.

As regards Sri Lanka's future I would strongly advise that when once the situation stabilises fresh elections should take place and Sri Lanka should have a Cabinet controlled government accountable to its Parliament with a President as its titular head having limited powers. Dynasty rule should be avoided at all costs. I am not prescribing any measures for its economic stability as I do not have full details on its economy.

14

TIME TO RETURN OUR DIAMOND

The continued exportation of our raw minerals to the UK is part of being a quasi-colony.

~

Vuyolwethu Zungula
President of the African Transformation Movement (ATM)

VUYOLWETHU Zungula, President of the African Transformation Movement (ATM), staunchly advocates for genuine sovereignty and challenges the traditional ties imposed by the Commonwealth, where membership requires an unwavering commitment to the Crown as the head. In a recent interview, Zungula expressed his rejection of this requirement, highlighting a fundamental disagreement with the notion that the head must always be the Crown.

One of the significant issues Zungula addresses is the historical exploitation of African resources, particularly the extraction of diamonds. He insists that returning these stolen diamonds is not just a symbolic gesture but a tangible act that would signify Britain's remorse for the past exploitation of African people and their resources. Zungula believes that such a gesture would contribute to healing the wounds of the past and building a more equitable relationship between nations.

As a Member of Parliament representing the ATM, Zungula emphasizes the importance of acknowledging and rectifying historical injustices. He contends that not only diamonds but all stolen minerals and artifacts must be returned to their rightful owners. This call for the repatriation of cultural and natural wealth underscores the broader theme of restitution and justice in the global context.

Vuyolwethu Zungula's stance reflects a commitment to reshaping international relationships based on principles of fairness, justice, and respect for the sovereignty of nations. By challenging established norms and advocating for the return of stolen resources, he contributes to a dialogue on historical reparations and the need for a more inclusive and just global community.

Excerpts of the interview;

Question: Tell us about the African Transformation Movement

(ATM) and its political vision to uplift the livelihoods of the country's people.

Answer: The ATM is grounded by the ideology of Humanism where we subscribe to the concept of One race for everyone, the Human race. The ATM is a values-based organisation and one of our chief values is UBUNTU. We believe that corruption is the absence of UBUNTU. All those who abuse taxpayers' money lack UBUNTU.

Q: You propose that South Africa withdraw from the Commonwealth while demanding "compensation for all damages done by Britain". Tell us why your country should leave the Commonwealth.

A: The ATM believes in genuine sovereignty. The fact that a deal breaker to be a member of the Commonwealth is that members must agree that the Head must always be the Crown. This to us means agreeing to be subjects of the British Monarchy. We reject that notion. The continued exportation of our raw minerals to the UK is part of being a quasi-colony.

Q: By endorsing the statement of known activist Thanduxolo Sabelo, you have reaffirmed that "the Cullinan Diamond must be returned to South Africa with immediate effect." Tell us more.

A: We are told that Queen Elizabeth was a champion of Decolonisation. Returning our Diamond will make us believe that Britain is remorseful for the exploitation of our people and our resources. All stolen minerals and other artefacts must be returned to the rightful owners.

Q: What is the next step if the British authorities ignore your request?

A: They shall have declared enmity on the African people and we shall continue with our campaign against the disguised colonisation.

Q: You are a dynamic and outspoken young politician in the country. Give us some thoughts on the current political situation and your plan to overcome the challenges.

A: The country under Ramaphosa and his administration has become a failed state. As ATM we have initiated an Impeachment or will continue advocating for a No Confidence vote remove Ramaphosa.

The ATM will work with other like-minded parties to Put South Africa 1st and rescue it from the failed state situation. The key to that is transforming the minds of South Africans so we get to work together in service to the country. South Africa must aggressively work on a localisation campaign where raw materials are processed in the country before being shipped to other nations, South Africa must produce what it consumes. The oligopolies dominating our economy must be dismantled to allow for more participation in the economy. With these, we believe poverty and unemployment would be tackled and South Africans would enjoy a better quality of life.

15

THE BRAINS BUSINESS

The Tamil Diaspora who are against Sri Lanka, came out of this 83 group.

~

Sampath Amaratunga
former Vice-Chancellor of the Sri Jayewardenepura University
and Chairman of the University Grants Commission

PROFESSOR Sampath Amaratunga, the former Vice-Chancellor of Sri Jayewardenepura University and current Chairman of the University Grants Commission in Sri Lanka, has emerged as a transformative figure in the country's higher education landscape. Known for his effective leadership style, Prof. Amaratunga has managed to instill discipline and warmth into the academic environment. A stark testament to his influence is the remarkable reduction in confrontations between students and law enforcement outside his office, a scenario that was once a daily occurrence.

In less than two years under Prof. Amaratunga's leadership, Sri Lanka is witnessing a profound transformation in its higher education sector. Plans are underway to establish City universities in 10 districts, repurpose campuses in the North and East into national universities, and establish entirely new institutions. This ambitious agenda signals a commitment to expanding access to education across diverse regions of the country.

In this interview conducted shortly after the challenging period of the Covid-19 pandemic, Prof. Amaratunga sheds light on why Sri Lanka's free education system is considered one of the best in the world. His insights provide a valuable perspective on the unique qualities that make the country's education system noteworthy and worthy of admiration. Through a blend of warm-hearted governance and an enthusiastic approach, Prof. Amaratunga appears to be steering Sri Lanka's higher education sector towards a future marked by inclusivity, accessibility, and academic excellence.

Excerpts from the interview;

Question: Let's start off about free education in this country, the challenges and the vision going forward?

Answer: It is because of free education that Sri Lanka has

enormous strength and growth. The largest resource for development is human capital. Equal benefits for all in education is important for the development of a country. An individual is given an opportunity (i.e education) and left with the option of taking it or leaving it. Only in Sri Lanka, do we have this free education system. I am a pure product of free education as I studied at Ananda College and went to Sri Jayawardenapura University.

Q: You recently mentioned the riots in 1983 where you remembered a song sang by your colleague. That year itself was a turning point in our country's history. Why is that memory etched in your mind?

A: I think it was a mistake, the war and the damage it had done, because the society had caused this riot. The opinion of the general public, even the international community is not favorable to Sri Lanka because of this original incident. The Tamil Diaspora who are against Sri Lanka, came out of this 83 group. It is a threat to peace and harmony today. They do not allow the South of the country to shake hands with the North and East. The children of this Diaspora follow their parents who were part of this 83 group.

Q: Undoubtedly education is one of the main ways to dispel these fears, as chairperson of the UGC how do you see this?

 A: We have a good network among the university system so we have to build trust. If you consider the University of Jaffna, that is a prime destination. The VC of the Jaffna university is a brilliant researcher who was nominated to the position many times but no one took notice. It was President Gotabaya Rajapaksa who arrived at this decision to appoint Sri Sathkunarajah as VC. Some spoke ill of him, but the President did not give in because Sathkunarajah is the right person for the right position. He is an important ambassador for peace.

In the South, universities have a huge tamil student population. In Sri Jayawardenapura and Colombo University we have more than 500 tamil students who peacefully coexist with others. Jaffna University has more than 1500 Sinhalese students. I don't see a better way to reconcile.

Q: Sri Lanka is often criticised in the international forum for its human rights records and lack of reconciliation efforts. If you factor in the education sector, how can we respond to that in a substantial manner?

A: We have to actively network and build on the trust between the North, South and East and the rest of the country. We have been engaged and we are successful. The government has announced the latest addition being the Gampaha Wickremarachchi Ayurveda University. The President's vision is to have a university in Vavuniya for which will soo be a reality. There will be much development in the area once you have a university in that territory.

Q: The issue of only a selected number of students being enrolled in universities remains. It is a highly competitive exam where only several thousand get through, and the others fall through the cracks. What is the alternative?

A: In 2018, we had 31000 students enrolled. By 2019, we increased this intake by 10 000, which is a 33 percent increase. This is the largest increase in intake. Yet another 140 000 students cannot enter national universities. We are therefore implementing many programs to facilitate them. We are enrolling 10 000 to the open university of Sri Lanka for Software engineering programs.

On the day they enroll we offer them a job. There are 40 000 vacancies in the IT sector in Sri Lanka. We have arranged an interest free loan for them for Rs.400 000 for a period of four years. We have also revisited all external degrees as it was a mess. We had allowed anyone to enter and do whatever they wished. We have rescheduled all arts degrees.

Q: There is this notion in Sri Lanka that students are closely engaged in union activities and spend their time and efforts on ragging and protesting. How are you going to tackle it?

A: I was the VC at Sri Jayawardenapura prior to my appointment here. Sri Jayawardenapura was once popular for student riots but I managed to settle the student population. During my time, I sat with them to discuss their issues. Similarly, if I came to know of their arrival to my office here, I would never leave until I sat with them and spoke to them. At times, I would meet them at the gate. That is because I am confident of what we are doing on the inside. They also know that if they come here, they always leave with an answer.

Q: There are claims that the quality of academia has been decreasing in the country and it is being widely reported in the media. What are the reasons and solutions to this?

A: I don't accept that notion. If you consider the total population, half the percentage of our output does not require any guidance. They are employable anywhere in the world, they don't come here to the UGC and neither do they request anything from us.

This is a percentage of the students who have transformed their skills set during the 3 or 4 years of studying. The rest of the students outside this high growth bracket are those who have failed to achieve some personal growth.

A student spends 12-13 years of school life before entering university. We don't know what kind of student is coming. We don't get to interview them. Nowhere else in the world can you enter a university without an interview except in Sri Lanka, thanks to free education.

The problem lies here. Yet this does not also apply to all faculties. Engineering, medical, and science are able to grasp things quickly. Those who do management leave with multiple qualifications. But when it comes to humanities and social sciences, 80 percent of them remain unemployed.

To this end we have taken several policy changes. The President wanted to us orient arts students with IT skills. It will be made compulsory for them to pursue IT and will be an added qualification. This way they will graduate with a double degree.

Q: I wanted to speak off the intellects who left our country for better opportunities. This brain drain, how do we put an end to this?

A: When a student pursues their higher education here and with the ample opportunities they are given, it is very likely they would receive a scholarship to a recognized institute overseas.

The reason we remain as a country lagging in economic growth is because of these selfish individuals. I feel that they must offer the country a service for the free education they have received. As soon as they finish a PhD their knowledge is still fresh and they can easily come back to offer their insight to the country or their own university. It can be in the form of new courses, new methodologies, research or technologies.

Q: What are the challenges you are facing because of the COVID pandemic?

A: Last year in March we closed all universities. The primary reason being the fact that our hostels have a huge student population residing and sharing open and public spaces such as canteens, libraries etc. So the risk was exponentially high.

The President wanted us to use this opportunity to activate

distance and online learning during this period. It was quite a challenge to bring everyone on board because we had not delivered a single lecture online prior to the pandemic. We have however accomplished it and have begun enrolling new batches as well.

Q: Recently you have introduced the concept of city university for an employable workforce. Please explain further.

A: I developed this city university concept and it is now under the leadership of Dr. Seetha Arambepola. The concept is mapped out for 10 districts in Sri Lanka in the first phase. In each of these localities we have conducted an extensive case study before the opening of the university in that particular district. For example in Kalutara, we assessed the types of industries, SME or large scale that are in operation. We then went to these places and inquired of the raw materials, technology, competency of the individuals working there and how we can help with the supply chain.

We then approached these industries and asked the managers if they would like to have a hand in the development of their district, if they would like to offer training to their workforce, whereby it will undoubtedly increase their productivity, efficiency and output. An official from the ADB upon hearing of this project told me this is one of the best rural development plans they have ever seen.

16

REJUVENATION IN THE NATIONAL PSYCHE

We have a very patriotic military.

~

Tareq Md Ariful Islam
High Commissioner of Bangladesh to Sri Lanka

IN AN INTERVIEW with Tareq Md Ariful Islam, the High Commissioner of Bangladesh to Sri Lanka, I had the opportunity to gain insights into his diplomatic journey and aspirations for the bilateral relationship between the two nations. Having assumed his duties in Colombo, Mr. Islam brings a wealth of experience to his current role. Prior to this, he served as the Deputy Permanent Representative in the Permanent Mission of Bangladesh to the United Nations in New York from 2016 to 2020, showcasing his dedication to international diplomacy.

A seasoned career diplomat, Tareq Md Ariful Islam joined the Bangladesh Foreign Service in 1998, and his professional trajectory reveals a commitment to various diplomatic assignments. Notably, he held the position of First Secretary/Counsellor in the Permanent Mission of Bangladesh to the United Nations in New York from 2005 to 2009. Subsequently, he contributed to diplomatic efforts in the Bangladesh Deputy High Commission in Kolkata, India, serving as Counsellor from 2009 to 2012.

The interview provides a glimpse into Mr. Islam's diplomatic journey and sheds light on his vision for fostering stronger ties between Bangladesh and Sri Lanka. His extensive experience in international diplomacy positions him as a key player in navigating complex diplomatic landscapes, and his dedication to advancing bilateral relations is evident in his previous roles and current responsibilities as the High Commissioner.

Excerpts from the interview;

Question: Please give me a brief profile of the country following its independence

Answer: We inherited a war-ravaged economy in 1971. But we were so fortunate to have a visionary leader like our Father of the Nation Bangabandhu Sheikh Mujibur Rahman. He immediately started building the country from the scratch. It is very unfortunate that he had only three and half years before he was assassinated in 1975. Yet in this short time, he put in place policy frameworks which gave us a strong foundational base. Subsequently, her able daughter our Hon'ble Prime Minister Sheikh Hasina took the helm and followed her father's footsteps. She went into a developmental overdrive, in particular from 2009. More importantly, she brought political stability in the country. As a result, today Bangladesh is considered a developmental miracle in the world. We have graduated to a developing country meeting all the UN threshold criteria.

We are having very consistent socio-economic development. Our socio-economic indices speak of it. Our GDP growth has been over 6% for the last 10 years, right before the pandemic it was 8.2%, one of the highest in the region. Even during pandemic, it was 5.8%, highest in Asia. Today, we are the 41stlargest economy in the world, going to be the 25thin 2035. This has been possible because the government relies on people's power. The focus has always been on helping and encouraging people to do things on their own. Pragmatic policy facilitation for growth created the right conditions for individuals to switch to entrepreneurial mindset and scale up. Graduates no longer focus on seeking jobs only, rather they go for self-employment and job creation. Our agriculture sector has done marvels, making us, a 170 million people living on 145000 square kilometers, self-sufficient in food. We have one of the best rice research institutes in the region which has developed high yield rice varieties. They can withstand adverse climatic conditions. Our service and industrial sectors are also coming up very strong. Our bigger story is about the resilience of our people which withstood countless adversities and brought us where Bangladesh stands now.

Q: You referred to the strategies in place that serve as an impetus for economic growth. What are they?

A: There were several strategic thrust areas. Let me mention a few. First, agriculture. Use of modern agricultural practices, new varieties of crops, cropping diversification, agro-processing have enabled this sector to flourish. We are now 4thlargest in the world in rice production, 5th in vegetable production, 4th in freshwater fish production and so on. The farmers no longer rely on traditional agricultural production only. They are going for other more profitable livelihood options and revenue streams, all surrounding agriculture. Greater road and digital/mobile connectivity enhanced marketability of their products. Technology has been a boon, farmers are not losing on middlemen since market prices are at their fingertips. Second, the power sector. Our Prime Minister herself oversees the Power Ministry. She took some bold and pragmatic steps due to which from a power deficit country we have turn into a power surplus country. Based on this, industry, ICT and service sectors developed. Third, women empowerment. Our Hon'ble Prime Minister, being a woman herself, made sure women are equal partners in the development of the country.

Our village women ventured into small businesses, from cattle rearing to cottage industries. In many households, women are breadwinners and decision makers. Their greater role took care of many other issues such as reducing child marriages and malnutrition, and ensuring education of their children which had a multiplier effect on the society as a whole. It changed the society's outlook towards women. Fourth, industry and service sector. Contribution of these sectors to our economy has surpassed that of agriculture. The manufacturing sector took off with the garment sector, there were many spin offs, backward and forward linkages which turned into a big industry. Uninterrupted power supply served as a huge booster to digitization of the economy based on which our service industry flourished.

As the economy improved, people's purchasing power did too. As a result, domestic demand and consumer market expanded significantly requiring various other industries such as electrical appliances, plastics to come up. Fifth, infrastructure. We invested hugely here. With boom in infrastructure development, rose our construction material industry such as cement, steel. There are also developments in other areas such as: expanding social safety net to lift the marginal section of the population from poverty, digitalization, opening up the private sector, public-private partnership, economic inclusion, which have made tremendous contribution to our economic rise. I can go on but would stop here.

Q: How do you get people to be committed to these policies?

A: People can make out which government is for the people and the poor. It didn't take our people long to find out which leadership is pro-people. When Prime Minister Sheikh Hasina took over, she knew, having undergone many hardships herself, the strength of her people. So, when people saw that her government was working for their best interest, was genuine in its intention and was delivering on its commitments, they gave all the support. The decisive factor behind Bangladesh's phenomenal success is that our Prime Minister has infused a sense of self-confidence in our national psyche often defying great odds. The US$ 3.7 billion Padma Bridge Project, which the government decided to fund from its own resources after the World Bank's withdrawal is a perfect example of that. That is why people are rallying behind this government.

Q: How does a government deal with citizens who are not equally confident and who take to social media to justify their allegations?

A: When the country is performing so well, there cannot be many complaints. But for any developing country, there will be developmental challenges and we also do. In any democracy, there will always be dissenting voices who would highlight the challenges only without acknowledging the country's and its people's achievements. The government is very much aware of the challenges and relentlessly trying to mitigate those. At the end of the day, what matters is what the majority of the people think. And here I believe we are on the right track.

Q: Tell us about internal security of the nation and how it fits into the larger picture of development?

A: Our tremendous socio-economic development has been the biggest catalyst of ensuring internal security. We are mostly a homogenous society which has been another factor. In our country, people of all faiths particularly the minorities have been living side by side in peace and harmony. So, we hardly have ethnic and communal issues posing threat to our internal security. In 2016, we had one terrorist attack and that came as an eye opener. That made us do a soul searching and the government took some pragmatic steps. We didn't look at containing terrorism from a security point of view alone. It has to come from society. So, while the security vigilance was on, we also adopted a 'whole-of-society' approach. Under that we activated a number of important actors in the society. First, mothers.

Our Prime Minister took it upon herself to call on mothers to be more alert about their children. Second, religious leaders. Religious leaders have significant influence on our society. So, we utilized them to guide and mobilize our people particularly the youngsters. Our Imams came up with counter-terrorism narratives in the light of the Quran and the Hadith which were widely disseminated. At the same time, we modernized our madrassa curriculum and aligned it with our mainstream education. As a result, students coming out of madrasas can sit for competitive exams and get any job they want to. There is no bar. All these worked very well and so far we haven't have any major terrorist incident. This is how we are ensuring our internal security. This has given a tremendous boost in carrying forward our development journey.

Q: How do you continue to attract FDI's into the country?

A: Ours is one of the most investment-friendly countries in the region. We have dedicated government bodies for attracting FDI and ease of doing business which come under the direct supervision of Prime Minister's Office. All necessary policies and framework have been put in place. Our developments in infrastructure and power sector have been a boon for FDI. We initially had a few export processing zones most of which were located close to ports and big cities. We are coming up with 100 Special Economic Zones (SEZs) across the country.

Now, you will find an SEZ even in a remote place of the country. This has been possible due to our good road and communication networks. Due to our very low production costs and availability of skilled human resources, we have become one of the most cost-efficient production hubs and outsourcing destinations in the world. Our increasing purchasing power and a surging domestic market of 170 million people is making large foreign companies invest in Bangladesh.

We have gone into car manufacturing with Honda and high-end cell phone manufacturing with Samsung, both of which have set up plants in our SEZs. Rapidly emerging private sector and a tremendous international export success are some of the other factors, which have led international companies to focus on Bangladesh. Number of Japanese companies in Bangladesh has tripled in last 100 years. During the pandemic, we have seen foreign companies relocating their operations to Bangladesh.

Q: In Sri Lanka we have had to face stiff opposition from people who take to the streets in protest over government's decisions. How about in Bangladesh, how do you manage this kind of scenarios?

A: Being a democracy, we also face similar situation. The

present government always listens to people's genuine demands and addresses them to the best of its ability. Environment and development, there is always a debateon which one to choose. We have to strike a balance. Bangladesh is a strong voice globally in addressing the adverse impacts of climate change, being a victim of climate change itself. Without waiting for international support, we have developed a climate fund from our own domestic resources to address our climate change related challenges. We have in place stringent mechanisms for environmental assessments. We are also working on greening our industries

Q: You also mentioned of your large diaspora. What role and how do they help in this process?

A: Our about 10 million strong diaspora play a huge role in our nation building. The foreign remittance that they send is the second largest source of our foreign currency earning. Initially, our manpower export was mostly about sending unskilled labour force to the Middle East. It is still there but we are now changing this by shifting to sending semi-skilled and skilled manpower. We have vocational training institutes all over the country. As we enjoy a demographic dividend of a large youth population, these institutions are turning them into efficient workforce. It's not only the number. We also have highly educated, technical professionals settled in North America and Europe. With these qualitative changes, our diaspora is making greater contribution to our development.

Q: During the last few years, you have been helping refugees who come into your country. How do you secure your border and assist them as well?

A: That has not been easy. But we had to. Having gone through the painful experience during our war of liberation when a large number of Bangladeshi had to take refuge in India, our Prime Minister decided that we must respond to the call of humanity.

No matter whether others do it or not. We may not be the best endowed but we have had the heart of taking up bigger responsibilities. It was a risky political decision because the opposition was criticising the government for opening the border. This time it was a bigger challenge due to the size of the influx.

The influx of forcibly displaced Rohingyas started with a small number and quickly snowballed to 1.1 million. We have in Cox's Bazar one of the world's largest camps. Maintaining such a big camp is not easy, the government has to allocate a lot of resources to help them. The international community has been very supportive. Particularly during this pandemic we need to be extra careful. But thankfully the rate of infection has been lower than the national average. Besides, it is not only about money, it is also about maintaining the law and order in the camps, containing the risk of radicalization as well as other unlawful activities which are easy to crop up in any camp situation. For any country, it's always a challenge. But our law enforcement agencies remain vigilant to address all the security implications. We seek the political support of Sri Lanka in resolving this crisis.

Q: Let us talk about the Sri Lanka and Bangladesh relationship.

A: I have some familiarity with the region, I served in Kolkata for four years. Then I looked after South Asia for another four years as Director-General from the Ministry of Foreign Affairs in Dhaka. During that period, I dealt with Bangladesh-Sri Lanka relationship. Bangladesh attaches high importance to her relations with Sri Lanka. When it comes to our relationship, it is all about friendship and goodwill. People here are very friendly and full of warmth. I feel comfortable being here. There are so many similarities between our two countries that I hardly feel that I am abroad. Age-old civilizational links and shared heritage, socio-cultural ties and people to people contact have reinforced the warmth of the relations. There a number of areas of cooperation which could bring significant gains to both countries. The large number of Sri Lankans working in Bangladesh is a strong element of our people-to-people contact. Bangladesh is committed to further strengthening and expanding these ties. My sole purpose is to pursue that.

Q: Prior to your appointment you were in the US. Tell us about your work there.

A: I have done a bit of multilateral diplomacy having been posted twice in the Permanent Mission of Bangladesh to the United Nations in New York. My area of work included international peace and security, human rights, regional cooperation and migration. In New York, I have seen first-hand how Bangladesh and Sri Lanka carry on their traditionally close cooperation in multilateral and regionalforums. We hold commonality of views on many global issues and extend support to each other. I personally worked closely with the Sri Lankan delegation in New York in upholding at the multilateral discourses the issues of our common interest.

Q: Most recently Bangladesh voted in support of Sri Lanka at the Human Rights Council. What was the reason for that?

A: I understand it was about the spirit of good neighbourliness. And, this is not new. We have been supporting Sri Lanka on human rights issues for many years now.

Q: Two days ago, Bangladesh offered a currency swap. Tell us more about that.

A: Swap arrangement was in fact conceived when Prime Minister Mahinda Rajapaksa visited Bangladesh in March this year. It was discussed and agreed in principle then. This currency swap is a follow up on that on the part of our Central Bank. We are happy to be of assistance to Sri Lanka. This again is about helping each other particularly the neighbours in hours of need.

Q: Given that all these nations are fighting a pandemic; how do you see regional cooperation?

A: Regional cooperation is very important. The pandemic has only reinforced the relevance and necessity of regional cooperation. We have two major regional bodies–SAARC and BIMSTEC and we need to put these two platforms to the best use. When developed countries themselves were struggling with the pandemic, most of them were not in a position to help us. Hence we, the developing countries, had to rely on ourselves. We are managing the most difficult pandemic in human history and that through our domestic efforts. You are also doing so. South Asia is not the most endowed region in terms of resources, here regional cooperation can help immensely. Pandemic management and vaccine could be the most important areas of effective regional cooperation. It is more about sharing best practices and experiences, and learning from each other.

Q: Looking ahead, how do you see diplomatic relations improving?

A: Our two countries have been enjoying excellent relations. The relationship at the political leadership level is particularly cordial. The visit of Hon'ble Prime Minister Mahinda Rajapaksa to Bangladesh this March to participate in the Birth Centenary of our Father of the Nation Bangabandhu Sheikh Mujibur Rahman and the Golden Jubilee of our Independence has been a high point of Bangladesh-Sri Lanka relationship. This has been a wonderful gesture of neighbourliness.

Now it's our duty to ensure that this political good will gets translated into sectoral cooperation in a more meaningful way. Trade and shipping are the two key areas of our cooperation, as I see it. Our bilateral trade volume is still small and does not commensurate with our excellent political relations. Both countries have their own comparative advantages and we need to couple these to our mutual benefit.

We need to take the trade to the next level. This would need some sort of trade facilitation and that could take various forms. To begin with, we are currently looking at preferential trade agreement (PTA) to explore our respective strong points and how we can help each other. Initially, we are looking at a small basket of items and if that works, we can expand and then move on to more comprehensive cooperation framework. Let me turn to shipping. As Bangladesh's economy is growing, so is our import-export. Our shipping connectivity with the rest of the world is naturally growing substantially. Our total container traffic stands at 3.2 million. I understand you want Colombo to be a bigger trans-shipment hub. We also want to shorten the freight travel time of our exports to the US and Europe. Here we have a win-win situation. So, we are working on some bilateral instruments in the shipping sector.

We are also working on several other bilateral instruments in investment promotion and customs cooperation which will have positive impact on our trade and shipping sectors. Pharmaceutical sector is another potential area of our cooperation since we have a big pharmaceutical industry exporting products to more than 80 countries including the US and EU. We also export pharmaceutical products to Sri Lanka but in relatively small quantity. It can be substantially increased. We are also planning to manufacture some of the vaccines as we have the capacity. Agriculture is a very important area of cooperation, where also we have done very well. We can share our best practices with you. Both the countries are doing very well in IT. Due to exponential growth of freelancing, Bangladesh is currently the number 2 in the world in IT outsourcing, after India. We can join our hands in this sector to enhance our global competitive. Tourism is another area. Particularly during the pandemic, when tourist flows from the West have trickled down, regional tourism taking advantage of geographical proximity can be a way to revive our tourism sectors. Maritime cooperation is one of our thrust areas. Being a maritime nation, you have long experience in long line and deep sea fishing. We can learn from that. So, you see, potential of cooperation between Bangladesh and Sri Lanka is huge for the mutual benefit of our people. So, in my opinion our relationship can only grow and flourish.

Q: In Bangladesh military officials are involved in national development in substantive manner. Can you tell us how do you use military while protecting the democratic norms and values?

 A: We have a very patriotic military. Apart from their primary responsibility of ensuring the security of the country, whenever there is a national crisis or priority, they are pressed into service in support of civil administration. We have seen it during natural disasters when the military works with people and others should-to-shoulder in disaster response and relief and rehabilitation. They are helping our law enforcement agencies during law and order situations. They are helping implement some national priority projects like building some major infrastructures, national ID Card, e-Passport etc. During the pandemic, they are working in the front line with our other front line workers. Our valiant soldiers are working as UN peacekeepers in conflict areas all around the world. We are now the number one troops and police contributor to UN peacekeeping. So, our armed forces are making invaluable contribution to our nation building activities.

Q: Tell us about the national Development policy framework promulgated by the Government of Bangladesh

A: Our Prime Minister have announced a number of plans: 'Vision 2021', 'Vision 2041', Vision of turning Bangladesh into a 'knowledge-based economy' and the 'Delta Plan 2100'. Vision 2041 aims to end absolute poverty and to graduate into higher middle-income status by 2031. It also aims at eradication of poverty on way to becoming a developed nation by 2041, the platinum jubilee year of our independence. We have adopted a Perspective Plan of Bangladesh 2021-2041', the second of its kind,to translate the policies and programmes into development strategies for 'Making Vision 2041 a reality. The institutional basis of this plan is fourfold, namely, good governance, democratization, decentralization and capacity building. The Strategic Goals and milestones of the Plan include industrialization with export-oriented manufacturing; paradigm shifts in Agriculture to enhance productivity; a service sector of the future-providing the bridge for the transformation of the rural agrarian economy to a primarily industrial and digital economy; the urban transition; efficient energy and infrastructure; building resilience to climate change and other environmental challenges; and establishing Bangladesh as a knowledge hub country. The Second Perspective Plan (2021-2041) would cover the periods of 8th, 9th, 10th and 11thFive Year Plans. It will also complement our efforts to achieving the global agenda – called Sustainable Development Goals (SDGs)by 2030 through the next two five year plans.

The Bangladesh Delta Plan (BDP) 2100 has the vision of "Achieving safe, climate resilient and prosperous delta". This is a techno-economic mega plan, first of its kind in the world that integrates all delta-related sector plans and policies, enveloping a Delta Vision and strategies that make it possible to integrate sector plans and policies for the long term and to present actionable interventions with a roadmap for realization.

With our people's support, we are confident of implementing all these visionary plans.

17

SRI LANKA AND TURKEY
NURTURING A WARM FRIENDSHIP

Turkey is home for around four million displaced people from different nationalities.

~

Demet Şekercioğlu
Ambassador of the Republic of Turkey to Sri Lanka

IN THIS insightful interview, I had the privilege of sitting down with Demet Şekercioğlu, the Ambassador of the Republic of Turkey to Sri Lanka. She shared a nuanced perspective on the historical diplomatic relations between Turkey and Sri Lanka, tracing the roots of this enduring connection back to the days of the Ottoman Empire.

Ambassador Şekercioğlu's detailed exploration shed light on the early engagements and cultural exchanges that marked the beginning of diplomatic ties between the two nations. With a focus on the Ottoman Empire's influence, she provided a historical context that showcased the foundations laid for a relationship that has weathered the test of time.

As the interview unfolded, Ambassador Şekercioğlu seamlessly transitioned to the contemporary scenario, offering valuable insights into the current social and economic landscapes of both Turkey and Sri Lanka. The discussion wove together historical threads with present-day realities, presenting readers with a holistic understanding of the diplomatic relations and the shared challenges and opportunities that continue to shape the bond between Turkey and Sri Lanka.

Excerpts from the Interview;

Question: It is said that diplomatic relations between Sri Lanka and Turkey extend to the Ottoman Empire. Can you briefly explain this fascinating history?

Answer: The rumor says that the first contact between the Turks and the people of the Island goes back to the 11th century, when Prince Cemaleddin (Jamaldden) from Konya came and settled in the Island in 1016. However, the diplomatic/consular relations between the Ottoman Empire and the then Ceylon are established in the second half of 19th century. In 1864, Mr. Hassan Lebbe Marikar is appointed as the Honorary Consul of the Ottoman Empire in Colombo. What is less known to the public is that the Ottoman Empire appoints also Mr. Sultan Bawa Jaman as its Honorary Consul in Galle in the same year. Beginning from that date, exchanges between the Ottomans and the Muslims of the then Ceylon will intensify.

In 1901, Honorary Consul Abdul Majeed actively takes part in the Silver Jubilee Celebrations of the accession of Sultan Abdulhamid II to the throne of the Ottoman Empire. To mark the occasion Consul Abdul Majeed lays the foundation stone of the new building of Al Madrasathul Khairiyyathul Islamiah which is the first Muslim boys' school founded in 1883 in Colombo. Later, the school's name will be changed as Hameediah School, in honor of Sultan Abdulhamid II. Among the legacies of Sultan Abdulhamid in Ceylon are the wearing of the fez cap and the display of the "star and crescent", which were the symbols of the Ottoman Empire. A street in the Hulftsdrop area in Colombo is named after the Ottoman Sultan as Abdulhamid Street.

Honorary Consul Mr. Abdul Majeed is succeeded by Sir Mohamed Macan Markar Efendi, who serves as the last Honorary Consul of the Empire in Ceylon from 1903 to 1915. He is initially the Honorary Vice Consul for the Ottoman Empire in Galle and later the Honorary Consul in Colombo. As the Turkish Consul in Ceylon, Mohamed Macan Markar visited Istanbul in 1909. Inspired from the Ottoman architecture, he will get a residence built at the heart of Colombo, he will name it after Istanbul "Villa Stamboul". The Street on which Villa Stamboul is located is called Stamboul Place even today.

Following the independence of Ceylon on 4 February 1948, the Embassy of the Republic of Turkey in New Delhi was accredited to Sri Lanka. From 1977 to 2000, Mr. Hema (Lofty) Wijeratne was the Honorary Consul General for the Republic of Turkey in Sri Lanka. In 2000, his daughter Mrs. Bharathi Wijeratne succeeded him to the position until she was appointed as the first Ambassador of Sri Lanka to the Republic of Turkey in 2012.

Q: You have served as a career diplomat in number of countries. How do you feel about being able to serve as the Turkish Ambassador to Sri Lanka?

A: I had the opportunity to serve in Rabat (Morocco), Lyon (France) and Brussels (Belgium) in the first years of my career, later I was appointed as Deputy Head of Mission to our Embassies in Kuwait and Islamabad (Pakistan). Before my ambassadorship, I served as Deputy Director General (DDG) for South Asia at the Ministry of Foreign Affairs in Ankara.

I considered myself privileged for being appointed as Ambassador to Sri Lanka for two main reasons. First, I was in charge of a number of countries including Sri Lanka as DDG for South Asia. I had the opportunity to visit Colombo back in May 2019, for the first political consultations held between our Deputy Minister, H.E. Ambassador Sedat Önal and the then Foreign Secretary of Sri Lanka, H.E. Ambassador Ravinatha Aryasinha. Therefore, I had already an acquaintance with the Turkish-Sri Lankan relations, which is always an advantage when one takes up a new mission.

Second, Sri Lanka is a very hospitable country with which we have a positive agenda. Both our people share common values, such as respect for human rights, freedom of speech and the rule of law. Sri Lanka just like Turkey is located at a strategic geography and is a mosaic of various religious, ethnic and cultural communities. Therefore, both countries also share similar challenges and struggles, which enabled us to develop mutual understanding and cooperation on issues of vital importance for our countries.

Q: Turkey has been a great support to uplift the lives of the people of Sri Lanka. Can you briefly describe your projects for human and physical development implemented in Sri Lanka?

A: Allow me first to correct a misunderstanding or

misperception about Turkey's humanitarian support to Sri Lankan people. From time to time, some allegations are voiced in local newspapers claiming that Turkey is funding/supporting some NGOs, groups or schools. I would like to once again underline the fact that Turkey does not directly transfer money to any party in Sri Lanka. We only work either with the Sri Lankan government or with NGOs, which are legally registered/recognized by the Sri Lankan state.

I also would like to remind here that the Republic of Turkey is a secular state, where there is a clear separation between religion and state affairs. The foundations of a modern legal system were laid in the early years of the Republic. Although the majority of the population is Muslim, Sharia law is not applied in Turkey. We also have a unified education system where the medium of teaching is Turkish. Turkey is a member of NATO, European Council, G20, as well as a candidate state to the European Union.

Particularly since the tsunami in 2004, Turkey has provided humanitarian aid, as well as development and capacity building assistance to Sri Lanka. In the past, we built 450 houses for the tsunami victims of 2004 in Matara; after the end of the civil war, we funded the construction of 100 houses in "Sri Lanka-Turkey Friendship Village" for the IDPs in Mannar; later we constructed a school, a playground and a hospital in the same village. Providing fishermen with fishing boats and other necessary equipment; renovating/building water tanks and water pumps, maintaining irrigation dams to support farmers; donation of 3D printers and laptops to universities, journalists; organising some training programs are among other activities carried out in the past through official Turkish aid agencies TIKA and the Turkish Red Crescent in a transparent manner.

Recently, we have donated twelve benchtop centrifuges, ten ventilators and other personal protection equipment to fulfil the requirements of the Sri Lankan health authorities in the fight against Covid-19. They were directly and respectively handed over to Honourable Minister of Health and to Honourable Foreign Secretary. Currently, we are working on distribution of dry food parcels for the most vulnerable people during the holy month of Ramadan.

We will continue our efforts, within our capacities, together with our Sri Lankan counterparts to see a more developed and stronger Sri Lanka in her region in the future.

Q: Like Sri Lanka, Turkey is a country threatened by separatist terrorists. What is the current policy of the incumbent President of Turkey to ensure national security and the safety of the public?

A: As you rightly mentioned, Turkey and Sri Lanka have been both subject to separatist terrorism. It is also striking to see the similarities between the two terrorist organizations, namely PKK and LTTE which target not only the territorial integrity but also the social fabric of our countries. PKK just as the LTTE began organizing in mid-seventies, it perpetrated its first terrorist attack in 1984. Abdullah Ocalan, the leader of the PKK, traveled to Syria in 1979 to receive military training, where he enjoyed safe haven until 1998. He was captured in 1999 by the Turkish Intelligence, in Nairobi (Kenya) where he was offered protection by the Greek Embassy. He is currently serving a life sentence in Turkey.

The PKK which has so far claimed over 40,000 lives is also involved in organized crimes such as extortion, arms smuggling, human and drug trafficking, to fund its terrorist activities. It also uses many of the means and tools elaborated by the LTTE, like abduction of children, use of child soldiers and female suicide bombers etc. Its objective is to suppress the diversity of Turkey, prevent its citizens of Kurdish origin to integrate in the social, political, economic and cultural life of the State. As such, it mainly targets infrastructures, facilities, schools, teachers, health personnel in the southeast of Turkey, causing more harm to our citizens of Kurdish origin, although it is claiming that it fights for their rights.

The PKK is not only present in Turkey; it has also offshoots and affiliates in our neighborhood, Iran, Iraq and Syria under various names. PYD/YPG which is operating in Syria shares the same leadership cadres, organizational structure, strategies and tactics, military structure, propaganda tools, financial resources and training camps as the PKK. The PKK is listed as a terrorist organization by various countries, including the members of the EU, the United States, Canada and Australia. However, PKK offshoot and affiliates largely exploit the democratic rights and freedoms in the West.

On the other hand, the PKK is not the only terrorist organization Turkey is fighting against. It will be recalled that on 15 July 2016, the Fetullah Gulen Terrorist Organization (FETO) tried to depose the democratically elected government of Turkey. This terrorist organization is at the same time a criminal and intelligence syndicate with global aspirations. While operating under the guise of a peaceful charitable organization and education movement, FETO aims at infiltrating into the state apparatus. Therefore, FETO poses a threat to the countries where it operates.

The presence of DEASH in our neighborhood also poses a serious threat to our national security. So far, more than 300 Turkish nationals lost their lives and 1,300 were wounded as a result of DEASH terrorist attacks. More than 1,100 DEASH affiliated terrorists, among whom more than half are foreigners, have been sentenced. Turkey is an active member of the Global Coalition against DEASH since its formation. It is co-chairing the Working Group on Foreign Terrorist Fighters. I deem it important to remind here that Turkey is actually the only NATO member that puts its troops on the ground to fight DEASH.

The developments achieved in our defense industry programs over the last years have played an important role in the success of our fight against terrorism. Today, Turkey is much less dependent on foreign procurements. We also continue to engage with our allies and partners to promote regional and international cooperation in putting an end to sinister and destructive activities of these terrorist organizations.

Q: Border tensions between Greece and Turkey are not new. What are the prevailing challenges in the area?

A: The Lausanne Treaty signed by both Turkey and Greece in 1923, among others, recognizes the boundaries of the newly established modern Turkey. It establishes a delicate balance between Turkey and Greece by harmonizing the vital interests of both countries including those in the Aegean. The basic thinking of the Treaty is to grant to coastal states (Turkey and Greece) limited areas of maritime jurisdiction and leave the remaining parts of the Aegean to the common benefit of both Turkey and Greece.

Thus, the Aegean is the common sea between Turkey and Greece. However, Greece regards the entire Aegean as Greek Sea. Therefore, while Turkey fully respects the provisions of the Treaty, since 1930's, Greece has been tilting to unilaterally extend its jurisdiction in the Aegean, and more recently in the Eastern Mediterranean, in total disregard of Turkey's rights and interests as one of the coastal states.

Many points of discord, which exist between Turkey and Greece have the same root cause and are interconnected. Various disputes like the delimitation of the Aegean continental shelf, air space related problems, militarization of Eastern Aegean Islands contrary to the provisions of the international agreements, as well as territorial waters breadth arise from the uncompromising attitude of our Greek neighbour. Let me clarify the situation for you by elaborating on a few points.

Greece extended its territorial waters from three miles to six miles in 1936 (Turkey followed the suit in 1964). Under the present six miles limit, Greek territorial sea comprises approximately 43.5 percent of the Aegean Sea, while Turkey's territorial sea is only 7.5 percent. The remaining 49 percent is high seas. If the breadth of its territorial waters were extended to 12 miles as claimed by the Greek side, Greece would acquire approximatively 71.5 percent of the Aegean Sea, while Turkey's share would increase to 8.8 percent. The Aegean high seas would diminish to 19.7 percent. Let me show you on the map what would be the consequences of such a move. If Greece extended its territorial waters to 12 miles, not only Turkey, but also third countries would clearly be denied the freedom of high seas in the Aegean.

Likewise, according to the maximalist position of Greece, all Greek islands in the Aegean and the Eastern Mediterranean automatically generate continental shelf and exclusive economic zones (CS/EEZ). Thus, Greece claims that a 10 km2 island (Kastellorizo), lying 2 km away from the Turkish mainland and 580 km away from the Greek mainland is supposed to create an area of 40.000 km2 CS/EEZ.

To sum up, you can clearly see on the map the CS/EEZ, Greece is accepting to concede to Turkey, which has the longest coast in the Aegean and Eastern Mediterranean.

I leave to the discretion of the reader to decide on the equitability and fairness of the intransigent attitude adopted by Greece. While Turkey is always advocating dialogue without any pre-condition to solve the existing bilateral issues with Greece, we have unfortunately once again witnessed their irreconcilable attitude during the joint press conference organized on the occasion of the official visit of the Minister of Foreign Affairs of Greece to Turkey on 15 April 2021.

Q: Turkey is the top shelter of humanitarian assistance to refugees coming from neighbouring countries. But, some Western countries criticize Turkey for not respecting democratic values and principles. May I have your response?

A: Turkey is home for around four million displaced people from different nationalities. More than 3.6 million of them are Syrians under temporary protection. We practically assume the responsibility of nine million Syrians, including those in Syria. We provide all kind of basic services to these people. We have spent more than 40 billion US Dollars for the well-being of Syrians and we continue our efforts to improve their living conditions.

There are more than one million school-age Syrian children in Turkey, over 750,000 of whom are currently attending school. The number of Syrian youth receiving university education in Turkish universities is around 37,000. Health-care is another sector where we continue our efforts. Until today, more than two million surgeries were conducted on Syrians. The number of Syrians receiving in-patient treatment exceeded 2.5 million. You can assess the size of the burden.

Despite all efforts of Turkey, millions of displaced people in the Northern Syria are still in despair due to the prevailing situation in Syria. Unfortunately, EU has turned a blind eye to our calls and appeals for equitable burden and responsibility-sharing. While Turkey has fulfilled her obligations stemming from 18 March 2016 Statement, and illegal crossings to Europe were reduced by 92% since 2015; the EU has yet failed to meet its commitments emanating from the same Statement. Refugee crisis is essentially an issue concerning Europe; no country can shoulder this burden alone.

In line with the related human rights instruments and 1951 Geneva Convention, every state has the obligation to receive asylum applications and offer international protection to those who are eligible. However, we see that Greece continues to push back and ill-treat asylum-seekers reaching its border. In the last four years, more than 80,000 migrants and asylum-seekers were pushed back to Turkey by Greece. It is also regrettable to see that the European Border and Coast Guard Agency, Frontex is deliberately helping Greek authorities to push migrant boats back, hence putting the safety of migrants at risk.

Certain circles unjustly accuse Turkey for backsliding on fundamental freedoms and erosion of the rule of law without taking into account the unique challenges Turkey continues to face. As I explained earlier, Turkey does not only shoulder the burden of four million asylum-seekers inside Turkey, and five million Syrians in Northern Syria, but is also under a considerable security threat emanating from its neighbour. Turkey pursues a simultaneous fight against multiple terrorist organizations operating within its territory and along its borders. Our fight against terrorism protects not only the basic human rights and dignity of our citizens and those of the millions of displaced people, but also the borders of the EU, where hostility against refugees, xenophobia, hate speech and Islamophobia are on the rise.

Q: Diplomatic relations between Sri Lanka and Turkey are improving day by day. In 2019, Turkey's trade volume with Sri Lanka was around $180 million. Tell us about future plans?

A: Although the Turkish-Sri Lankan relations have a deep history dating back to the 19th century, the visit of His Excellency President Recep Tayyip Erdoğan as the then Prime Minister of Turkey on 10 February 2005, in the context of his tour to the countries affected by the 2004 tsunami marks a threshold in our bilateral relations. Turkey lent a helping hand to Sri Lanka's efforts to overcome challenges caused by the tsunami. The warming relations were followed by high-level visits and the opening of the Embassy of Sri Lanka in Ankara and our Embassy here in Colombo, respectively in 2012 and in 2013. Since then, our relations have been steadily developing in a cordial atmosphere. My mission in Colombo is to further deepen and strengthen both the government-to-government and people-to-people ties for the mutual benefit of our people. We have a number of mechanisms and tools we can use to this end.

One of the most important tools is the Turkey-Sri Lanka Joint Economic Commission (JEC) which was established back in 1988. We revived this mechanism through the meeting held on 11-12 November 2016 in Ankara. The second meeting, which was scheduled to take place in Colombo at the end of May 2019, has been postponed due to the tragic Sunday Easter Attacks and later due to the pandemic, which took the World hostage last year. We are now hoping to hold it, at the earliest appropriate time, to review the whole range of our economic and trade relations and to discuss the ways and means to overcome the impact of the pandemic together.

After the opening of our Embassies, Turkey-Sri Lanka bilateral trade figures have progressively increased up to 229 million USD in 2018. During this JEC of 2016, a goal of 500 million USD was set to be achieved by 2020. Unfortunately, the unexpected developments of those last years did not allow us to reach this goal. Yet, there are positive developments that enable us to be optimistic.

Turkey became top tea importer of Sri Lanka in 2017, and except in 2018, she continues to occupy the first rank. Turkey's flag carrier, Turkish Airlines (THY) has been operating passenger and cargo flights between Istanbul and Colombo since 2013. The flight frequency was seven times per week before the pandemic. Although passenger flights were suspended for a short while, continuing its cargo flights, THY has undertaken an undeniable task to deliver Sri Lankan goods to the world market. THY's passenger fights are currently operating five times per week, and offering an immense service to the revival of the Sri Lankan tourism sector, as well as to the development of people-to-people relations between Turkey and Sri Lanka.

The Turkey-Sri Lanka Business Council of the Foreign Economic Relations Board of Turkey has been organising regular online webinars to bring together the business communities from Turkey and Sri Lanka during the pandemic. Its members are also very keen to visiting Sri Lanka, to discover the business opportunities on the site, as soon as the conditions permit. I am glad to observe that despite the pandemic, some Turkish business people were willing to invest in various sectors in Sri Lanka. Direct capital investments from Turkey to Sri Lanka are estimated to be around 3 million US Dollars. Considering the potential of both countries, there is ample room to increase this figure. Of course, Sri Lanka should do its share of the work to realize this by easing doing business climate in the country.

Last but not least, the establishment of the Sri Lankan-Turkish Inter-parliamentary Friendship Association within the Sri Lankan Parliament last March, is also a step forward to enhance relations between the representatives of our people, which will certainly contribute to the existing cordial relations.

18

OUR RELATIONS ARE ON A POSITIVE TRAJECTORY

Pakistan's Armed Forces, highly professional and adaptable, evolve responses to counter a dynamic spectrum of threats.

~

Muhammad Saad Khattak
Pakistan High Commissioner to Sri Lanka

MAJOR GENERAL (Retd) Muhammad Saad Khattak, Pakistan High Commissioner to Sri Lanka, emphasized the critical role that South Asian countries play on the global stage, constituting a staggering one-fourth of the world's population. Despite this demographic significance, he highlighted a concerning paradox – the region's notable lack of integration when it comes to regional cooperation. This observation, made during an exclusive interview conducted a few months before his tenure in Sri Lanka concluded, sheds light on the challenges faced by South Asian nations in fostering collaborative efforts for mutual benefit and progress.

Major General Khattak's illustrious career spans over three decades, marked by diverse assignments both within and outside the borders of Pakistan. His academic background, including graduation from the French Army Junior Staff Course, Defense Intelligence Directors Course in the UK, and completion of programs at prestigious institutions like the Command and Staff College Quetta and the National Defence University Islamabad, underscores his commitment to continuous learning and professional development. With Masters Degrees in Political Science and War Studies, along with an M. Phil in International Relations, he brings a wealth of knowledge to his diplomatic role.

Having confronted the complex challenges of Counter-Terrorism in Balochistan and Khyber Pakhtunkhwa/FATA, Major General Khattak gained invaluable insights during his senior positions in Islamabad/Rawalpindi. His unique experiences provide a firsthand understanding of the ongoing efforts against terrorism and contribute to his nuanced perspective on the intricate dynamics of the War on Terrorism in the region.

Excerpts from the interview;

Question: You have earned around 35 years of an illustrious career in various assignments both inside and outside Pakistan.

First of all, I We would like to know, what triggered you to join the military?

Answer: In our society Military has traditionally been seen as a profession of great respect and merit. Few members of my family had joined before me who also served as motivation for my opting to join Army. Moreover, as young students we were always under the illusion that the early you join military, the early one would get rid of formal education which later proved a fallacy as in the military one goes through so much of academic and professional education that far surpasses formal academic education in the universities.

 Q: Like many other countries, the military as an institution is one of the strongest state apparatus in Pakistan. You were a senior military officer who worked at various places of the country. What are the emerging threats and how does your military help to measure them to implement a proactive mechanism which will prevent any hindrance to social order?

A: Pakistan Armed Forces are one of the most professional outfits in the world. With the dynamic spectrum of threats, the responses of the institution are also evolving to counter the challenges. Pakistan Army has proved its metal and strength in successfully overcoming present day challenges including terrorism, disaster management and effectively assisting the government in combating the Covid-19 pandemic. It is the success of Pakistan Army and government of Pakistan as a whole that Pakistan stood 3rd, world over, in post pandemic recovery according to "The Economist's Covid-19 Normally Global Index".

 Q: You are a military expert turned diplomat. How did you incorporate your military experiences with diplomacy?

 A: Given the evolving dynamics across all fields, no one in the first place can claim to be expert of any field. During the course of higher military education, we are exposed to various aspects of Diplomacy, be it defence, economic or public diplomacy. Practical application and manifestation of knowledge gained to a very dynamic environment like Sri Lanka has been a unique honour and privilege for me. Besides, as soldiers and senior commanders we are trained in human handling, across different cultures, utilizing the art of negotiations and interactions through effective communication skills that we learn over years of experience. Honestly, despite the restraints of Covid- 19 over the last almost 2 years, I have been able to meet and interact with all segments of Sri Lankan society across the entire nook and corner of the country that has added a great deal to my learning besides further strengthening our mutual bonds. I am highly indebted to the Sri Lankan leadership and people for their whole hearted support.

Q: Both Sri Lanka and Pakistan are members of a few regional bodies such as SAARC. Regional cooperation is vital to any country for achieving its goals. We would like to have your take on the prevailing situation of regional operation between South Asian countries and the challenges ahead? How can we overcome those challenges?

 A: South Asian countries together comprise 1/4 of the world's population. This region, however, is the least integrated in terms of regional cooperation. SAARC has remained hostage to India's bullying policies and desire to maintain regional hegemony over her smaller neighbours. Since India is the largest country in the region so unless it shows maturity, the region will remain hostage to poverty and underdevelopment. The world has felt a dire need for regional and multilateral integration post COVID-19. If we want to overcome these challenges, we need to strive for equality in mutual relationship to exploit our full potential for regional integration and development. In this regard China has recently launched a new initiative by the name China-South Asian Countries Poverty Alleviation Initiative. Five out of seven countries who are already part of BRI have shown their willingness. India and Bhutan are so far silent. This initiative of China has tremendous potential to improve mutual trade promising greater integration of the region.

Q: Pakistan is one of the trusted partners of Sri Lankans to improve their skills in many subjects, most importantly education and security. You have helped Sri Lanka during the brutal war against terrorism that lasted three decades. We would like to know more detail about this collaboration.

A: Pakistan launched Pakistan-Sri Lanka Higher Education Cooperation Programme for Sri Lanka with the capital cost of approximately US$ 18.402 million. Under this programme, 800 fully funded and 200 partially funded scholarships are being offered to Sri Lankan students at graduate, post-graduate level. Under this arrangement, Allama Iqbal Scholarships have already been launched. 50 selected students are currently undergoing studies in Pakistan under this program in the field of engineering, basic & natural sciences and social & management sciences. During his visit to Sri Lanka earlier this year, the Prime Minister of Pakistan announced 100 special medical seats for Sri Lankan students in addition to the 1000 scholarships already being offered. Moreover, process for 250 seats for the year 2021-22 has been initiated. This program will greatly help in enhancing people-to-people contacts between the two countries.

The Government of Pakistan is also giving Jinnah Scholarships to Sri Lankan students for the past 14 consecutive years where top scoring O/Level and A/Level Sri Lankan students receive monetary handouts. So far, 2000 Sri Lankan students have benefitted from this scheme.

Moreover, Defence ties between Sri Lanka and Pakistan are time tested and built on a strong foundation. This bond is further strengthened after 2009 when Pakistan provided its unflinching moral and material support to Sri Lanka in LTTE War.

This ever-growing defence relation is based on Capacity building of the Sri Lankan Armed Forces through training and provision of modern day military hardware. Pakistan provides over 600 vacancies annually to Sri Lankan armed forces on gratis basis in various training institutions of Pakistan. Both the country's armed forces participate in bilateral as well as multinational exercises.

Q: There are untapped areas in Pakistan and Sri Lanka yet to be explored, such as food production, tourism, and pilgrimage. Please let us know your plan to identify the potentials of these areas to enrich diplomatic relationships?

A: Both countries are tourists hotspots which could not be fully exploited due to security situation in the past few decades. Whereas Sri Lanka is home to beautiful beaches and natural beauty, Pakistan besides its beautiful coast offers a variety of attractions like the beautiful virgin Northern Areas, Swat etc. Remains of ancient civilizations like Mohengo-Daro, Harappa and Buddhist religion are attractive spots for interested tourists from the world. The other common ground to visit our countries is the cultural and sports ties between the two countries while promotion of religious tourism can further bring the two nations closer to each other. Moreover, we are in the process of launching a documentary film on the glorious Gandhara Civilization and Buddhist heritage of Pakistan. We are in touch with the Sri Lankan Prime Minister's Office for the joint launch of this documentary. It will further boost the understanding and friendship of the two countries as well as acrossall the Buddhist countries in the world.

A number of initiatives have been taken to improve bilateral trade between two countries during recent years. Three editions of the Pakistani Single Country Exhibitions have been organized in Sri Lanka during 2016, 2017 and 2018, which translates into higher volumes of bilateral trade. The High Commission of Pakistan in Colombo also held the first virtual business forum in collaboration with Sri Lanka Export Development Board (SLEDB) to enhance awareness regarding trade and investment opportunities under the Pakistan Sri Lanka Free Trade Agreement between the two friendly countries on 18th September, 2020. More than 100 companies from both sides participated in the Webinar and the event was a great success. A series of sectors-specific webinars and business forums have been planned for the next six months with public and private stakeholders from both sides across sectors such as Construction materials, pharmaceuticals, textiles, information and communication technology and Buddhist tourism development in Pakistan. Steps are being taken to facilitate Buddhist tourism from Sri Lanka to Pakistan, so that people can experience our rich Buddhist heritage as well.

The Trade and Investment Wing of High Commission of Pakistan, in collaboration with Ministry of Commerce and Trade Development Authority of Pakistan (TDAP), organized a promotional event for Pakistani Dates (Fruit) Exports in Sri Lanka, at the High Commission in Colombo on 08th April 2021.

Following the recent visit of the Prime Minister of Pakistan to Sri Lanka, a high-level 14-member Buddhist Monks' delegation visit has been arranged by High Commission of Pakistan in Colombo during April 2021 to promote religious tourism to Pakistan and to enhance people-to-people contact between Pakistan and Sri Lanka.

Q: Pakistan is the second-largest trading partner of Sri Lanka in South Asia. Sri Lanka was the first country to sign a Free Trade Agreement with Pakistan, which became operational in 2005. We believe both countries have a long road ahead. What are the plans to improve trade and the economy?

A: After the signing of Pakistan Sri Lanka FTA in 2005, exports from Pakistan to Sri Lanka have seen an increase from US$ 100 million to US$ 369 million in 2019, but the mutual trade remains much below the potential. Exports from Sri Lanka to Pakistan have also witnessed a surge from US$ 46 million in 2005 to US$ 105 million in 2018. However, the figure has dampened to US$ 81 million in 2019, which can be attributed to the local economic and security challenges faced by Sri Lanka in the last year. The High Commission of Pakistan is fully committed to increasing bilateral trade under the FTA. We are in close coordination with the relevant Sri Lankan authorities in order to strategize enhancing Sri Lanka's exports to Pakistan. Through a number of measures such as encouraging Sri Lanka-specific trade exhibitions in Pakistan, arranging buyer delegations from Pakistan for B2B engagements, organizing business forum and raising matters related to tariff and non-tariff barriers being faced by Sri Lankan exporters with Pakistani authorities.

Pak-Sri Lanka bilateral trade has the estimated potential of over US$ 2 billion. Some of the potential export products from Pakistan are Portland cement, denim fabric, woven fabric of cotton yarn, medicaments & surgical instruments, paper & paper boards, articles of silk & synthetic textile, knitwear, fertilizers, towels, bed wear, cutlery, leather products, sports gears and footwear. Top import products from Pakistan to Sri Lanka are Vegetable products and Betel Leaves, Coconut and Copra, Fiber boards, Natural Rubber and Tea. Sri Lanka's exports to Pakistan only has a share of 0.7% in Sri Lanka's total exports. A range of new products have also penetrated into the Pakistan market after the implementation of the PSFTA and these new products include items such as fresh pineapple, MDF boards, tamarind with seeds, edible oil, porcelain tableware & kitchenware, ceramic tiles, furniture, electrical switches & sockets, herbal cosmetic products, plastic articles, paints, glass paintings, leather products, frozen fish, prawns, lobsters, crabs, cut flowers & foliage and gems & Jewellery.

Q: Pakistan and Sri Lanka have maintained a very cordial diplomatic relationship since the beginning. Can you give us a brief outline of this strong diplomatic relation between the two countries?

A: Since the establishment of diplomatic relations between Pakistan and Sri Lanka in 1948, the two countries have maintained a close, cordial and mutually supportive relationship. We have been helpful to each other during difficult times and always coordinate our positions on regional and international fora. Our relations are on a positive trajectory however, Pakistan wishes to expand its economic, trade, defence and cultural relations with Sri Lanka.

19

PERSPECTIVES OF AN EMINENT PUBLIC SERVANT

Once you build a family, let there be harmony, start building a house in a small way, try to live within your means.

~

Lalith Weeratunga
Former Permanent Secretary to the President of Sri Lanka

PRINCIPAL Advisor to President Gotabaya Rajapaksa sat with me at his tiny simple but neat office room at the Presidential Secretariat in Colombo to outline the needs of structural reforms in the Sri Lanka Administrative Service. He narrated his experiences as a young enthusiastic administrative officer in the late 70s Sri Lanka's as well as the President's vision for economic and social revival of the country, particularly in rural areas.

Lalith Weeratunga served as the Secretary to the President of Sri Lanka between November 2005 and January 2015. He entered the Sri Lanka Administrative Service (SLAS) in January 1977 and has held a number of senior positions in the public service as the Secretary to the Prime Minister, Additional Secretary to the Ministry of Education & Higher Education, Director General of the Tertiary and Vocational Education Commission and Vice Chairman of the National Apprenticeship Board. He was also the Chief Technical Advisor/Vocational Training Specialist in the Regional Office of the International Labour Organization (ILO) for Asia & Pacific, and had worked as a Consultant of the United Nations Development Programme for the Government of Maldives. Throughout his career, he has served in a number of Governing Councils of Universities, and Boards of Directors of Public Corporations and Statutory Boards.

Mr Weeratunga received his primary education from Rahula College, Matara before entering the Royal College, Colombo for his secondary education. He holds a Masters Degree in Business Administration from the University of Colombo and a Bachelors Degree in Natural Sciences from the same university. Later, he attended the Pennsylvania State University for postgraduate studies. He is a Hubert H. Humphrey Fellow of the Pennsylvania State University, USA.

Q. Can I know what led you to join the Sri Lanka Administrative Service (SLAS) as far back as 1977 and what was it like back then?

A. I think it was because I had a liking to join the public service. I joined as a SLAS cadet through the open competitive exam. The administrative services at the time were well set so you knew the parameters under which you could work; one couldn't do as they wished.

One inherits all that was established by the British including the system. My entry was on the notion that I could contribute more. I came from the private sector where I had more perks and higher salaries but I realized, being in the public service meant I could do more. At the same time, my parents were teachers and I hailed from a background which also led me to join the public service.

There is a saying that the private sector is the primary engine of growth, which may be true, but for it to be the primary engine, the public sector has to hold the system together. That is why in countries like India, the public sector is so strong that no person, politician or individual can tamper with it. Even to date people say it is the Indian Administrative Service which governs the country and not the politicians.

In 1972 when the Public Service Commission (PSC) was abolished, the then politicians at the time made the PSC, functionally retarded. The public service of Sri Lanka before then earned the reputation for being the best in the whole of Asia. But we lost it over time with political interference. Consequently, it became something one could tamper with. I am not saying that the public service must be kept completely independent and aloof, but if the public servant does not respect the politician, and vice versa there is no harmony. It is this harmony that keeps the balance. Politicians must also respect and realise that these are people who are capable and qualified. As long as that balance is there, governance of the country will be good.

Q. What do you see as being the reason for this looseness?

A. I think both politicians and the public is to be blamed. If politicians begin to unduly interfere there is an issue. On the one hand, if development projects are being delayed by public servants then the politician has all the right to question. On the other, if the politician wants something done by violating an established procedure such as a recruitment based on loyalty, it cannot be done.

Q. Do you think the decades-long armed conflict has had an impact?

A. Somewhat. At one time Jaffna had a Sinhalese Government Agent, Trincomalee had a Sinhalese Government Agent and there were Tamil Government Agents down South, it assured that communities were blended.

But when you have a GA catering to one ethnic community, where is the harmony then? It sows division. I think the conflict would have had an impact because at the time of war Sinhalese could not work in the North or the East. Qualified individuals could not be recruited. There were unqualified individuals and entry requirements were relaxed only for the North and East. The training component was also compromised.

Now we have ad hoc programmes. You can be told how to do your work but you also need to be taught how it's done. From birth to death, you need to deal with the government at every step. If I am rude to you, it may impact your impression of the government. Today, unfortunately, the public sector feels that they are the masters not the servants. When we received our letters of appointment at my time one condition was that we had to work wherever we were transferred. We could not even choose our place of work.

Q. During your time you tried to reengineer and redesign the administrative system.

A. It was called the reforms council, although I don't want to take credit, I was a pioneer in looking for a new system, and ways to modernize. What we inherited from the British was old, the internet was available and we had to make use of this technology. I was also the first Director of the re-engineering component at the Information and Communication Technology Agency (ICTA). We were able to do many things, like issuing a birth certificate within a few minutes. Governments need to enact reforms but changing people is difficult. We wanted to make things simpler, for instance the forms, why do we need so many forms? The government must know those details rather than asking the citizen for it. Attempts were made for change but there was resistance. You need an understanding of a modern government, to make an administrative system work better and faster. What the President wants to do is to have a digitized and modernized government that is also people friendly.

Q. Many people talk about red tapes in the administrative system

A. The word red tape stems from the bureaucracy. It is a concept of who has power and not of delay. However, red tape is now linked with unnecessary delays. When they say there is too much of 'bureaucracy', it generally means too much of delay. If you go back to the time when people had to go to the bank to cash a cheque, they had to go in the morning and come back many hours later. Then they say it's 'bureaucracy' but when you bring in technology, there is no delay. For the ordinary person at the village level, 'bureaucracy' means having to go to the government office multiple times to get one job done. Why can't that officer once and for all, ask what needs to be provided? Even in the best system you can still have 'bureaucracy'. Technology can remove these delays.

Governments are there to offer solutions and to also maintain a system. There is a commission appointed by the President which I am chairing, and we are tasked with seeing how we can streamline these processes.

Q. You have worked with the United Nations Development Programme (UNDP) in Maldives and as the chief technical advisor/vocational training specialist in the regional office of the International Labour Organization (ILO) for Asia & Pacific, Thailand. How have those experiences been?

A. At a young age when you are exposed to international management it really adds to the exposure and it enabled me to get a global perspective. How one works with foreigners and in the international scene is very important to understand how we can improve our systems and the way we can contribute for national endeavors. I learnt new ways of doing things.

Q. As you mentioned your international work gave you exposure, do recruits now have the same opportunity?

A. Certainly, there are enough and officers should seek them out. It is up to the officers to sharpen their skills. I am someone who believes that I don't have any competitors. I always compete with myself. It all depends on how you do your job to the best of your ability. I think people must learn to set their own standard and reach it. That standard must come from reading and learning from others. I always say to sharpen one's skills and not rest on your laurels. I think you need to keep on learning, but it's not a matter of the number of Degrees that you have. It is learning, not about a piece of paper.

Q. Tell us about your day. How do you schedule your day?

A. I am at an age where I try to take it easy. I am doing a job that is voluntary so I am relaxed. I walk for about 6 to 7 kilometers every morning. I am somehow working a lot at home, so I help my wife. I believe that the family is a joint effort; you must help each other under any circumstances to make things and situation comfortable to each other for a long and meaningful journey. I also enjoy gardening and it keeps me busy.

Q. What is your advice to young public service officials and others in the public sector?

A. The first is to never have competitors but to compete with yourself. They also say to have goals, but I looked at the learning process. Once you build a family, let there be harmony, start building a house in a small way, try to live within your means. Have qualities that will make people want to approach you.

Q. As the Principal Advisor to the President, you are actively participating with the Gama Samaga Pilisandara (Dialogue with the Village). Can you outline the objectives of this programme?

A. The President didn't suddenly wake up and decide to meet villagers. He has been doing it for the last four years. He would have gone to almost all parts of the island but in the process he realized that there are very remote villages with no proper schools, roads, and other basic requirements for a normal decent life.

A lot of barriers for irrigation, mismanaging the environment, acquiring of farming lands by the forest department with no prior notice. He realized the magnitude of the land issue. You can't give lands to everybody but to at least those who cultivate. Having seen the existing mechanisms and issues, the President realized the expectations of the people that have not been met for a long time. Since independence to date, there had been villages that had not seen any senior politicians or senior government officials.

This is a revolutionary development programme. The President can easily get all the Divisional Secretaries, Ministers together and direct them.

But how much of it will be done, how does he monitor? He gives people the opportunity to come and tell him directly what their needs are. These are what he needs to hear from the villagers so he can see the depth of it gravity of their problem. And the way we have selected the villages through the law enforcement agencies, political system, and divisional secretariats it gives him the chance to go to the most remote villages. And then we prepare the meeting with the people and give people free access to him (?).

There is an allegation that these questions are planted. You can't plant questions like that. People are standing up randomly. If the question is planted by a politician it will be to his benefit but in this programme the people demand solutions and blame the politicians. When the President goes to the village, the Health Secretary goes and he sees the condition of the hospitals. It is the same with the other Ministry Secretaries such as Education, Agriculture or Irrigation. They see what needs to be done, first hand.

If the system works so well the President does not have to go to the village. So he goes there and gets it done. When you see ground level issues he can formulate policies better. If the President had not gone there at all, nothing would have happened. Not just in that Division but in the adjoining Divisions as well. For the Presidential visit, there is preparatory work done as well. Previously those who have gone to villages have done so with much fanfare, but it's not the same here. All in all, there is a huge impact because of his visit there is so much that is achieved.

During the President's first visit to Haldummulla we found out that there were many houses without electricity and now when we review the progress we find that so many have been achieved since his visit, including providing electricity. As soon as he gets into a the helicopter he gets a report which says what has been discussed. That is done by a team who goes there earlier. We are aware of what we are tackling. New issues may come up at the time. The President also decided to donate 500 books to schools during every visit, as these are remote villages. I personally select those. Gama Samaga Pillisandara is a revolutionary village development initiative where the President goes to the village by himself to listen and understand as well as take and implement the decisive actions to achieve a decent livelihood for all.

Q. Tell us about the environmental issues that are in the headlines these days?

A. The President needs to go and see for himself what has happened to the village. There are instances where the Forest Department has taken over farming lands in the village. Even in the forest, you need to keep the core area but if people are not given the cultivation area, there is a bigger challenge. While maintaining the forest area, you need to allow people to do cultivation around those areas. Some people with vested interests have taken advantage and said that after this government came into power, deforestation has increased. My argument is that there are forest officials, wildlife officials who are tasked with looking after the forest. But the government has the responsibility to ensure that people's lives are maintained. These villagers are also not the ones who destroy the forest, people in the village look after the forest because they know the value of it. We can't deny that the mass scale deforestation is that has been done by businessmen and corrupt politicians for many decades now. People want land for livelihood. Ordinary people in those areas protect the forest It is part of their tradition. Colombo based pseudo-critics do this only on social media, and it goes viral but the truth is that people need something to live on.

Q. What is your message to people those who are using social media and other means to voice their negative criticism?

A. Everybody has fundamental rights to criticize after ascertaining the facts. If you can't see it for yourself, send someone there to check it for you. Then raise your argument to change for the better.

Q. In conclusion, we would like to have a glimpse of the President's vision for the country since you are voluntarily offering your service as his Principal Advisor.

A. The President's vision is very clear in the national framework, and it has so many activities which need to be progressed by each of these ministries. His vision for the country is that he wants a country where people can live without any fear or suspicion and a country where we have minimized poverty and having a decent livelihood. He wants children particularly to be technologically advanced. No matter what school they go to, it is very important that they have the technology to update their knowledge. His vision, as he himself says, is a secure country. If there is no security, there is no development. He wants to build a country where there is a happy family.

20

NUANCES OF
PEDAGOGICAL MISSION

Organizational management hinges on forecasting, planning, implementing, and monitoring resources.

~

Sivakolundu Srisatkunarajah
Professor in Mathematics and Vice Chancellor of University of Jaffna

PROFESSOR Sivakolundu Srisatkunarajah, the current Vice Chancellor of the University of Jaffna, stands as an exemplary figure in the field of education, showcasing a remarkable ability to guide the institution towards a future of excellence. His rich blend of skills and experience allows him to effectively leverage both human and technical resources, fostering an environment conducive to academic growth. His visionary leadership is underscored by a commitment to innovation and a well-established strategic direction.

During a recent meeting held in his office at the university, I had the privilege of engaging in a lengthy discussion with Srisatkunarajah. Throughout our conversation, he expounded upon his vision for the institution and emphasized the profound impact education can have on shaping the future of the country. His deep-rooted belief in harnessing the inherent power of the university to produce world-class intellects echoes his dedication to driving positive change.

Born in the early 60s, Srisatkunarajah embarked on his academic journey at Jaffna University in 1979, where he pursued a degree in mathematics and graduated with first-class honors. His academic pursuits led him to complete his PhD at Heriot-Watt University, Edinburgh Campus in 1988, where he delved into groundbreaking research on the asymptotics of the Heat equation for polygonal domains.

As a distinguished educator and pioneer in mathematical theories, Srisatkunarajah's overarching objective is to transform the lives of students and communities through education, learning, and knowledge creation and dissemination. His commitment extends beyond meeting market demands, as he envisions an education system that not only imparts knowledge but also molds students into responsible citizens.
Following are the excerpts of the interview;

Q. Tell us in briefly of your vision and activities you have undertaken to achieve your vision as a Vice Chancellor of this university?

A. As the leader of the University, in my policies and actions, I adhere to the highest standards of professional integrity. I will promote critical enquiry and the rational evaluation of evidence, among my peers, even if such an approach leads me to reevaluate my own decisions as Vice Chancellor. I will at all times place the institution of the office of the Vice Chancellor above that of the individual holding the office.

I rigorously promote and evaluate the effectiveness of the teaching and learning support provided to students, the quality of campus social and cultural life, the originality and relevance of research to sustain and continually reinforce the academic quality of our degree programmes, and ensure that students gain maximum educational and social values.

Staff are the core resource of a University. University of Jaffna will be able to produce excellent research and will provide students with the very best learning opportunities only if the University can attract, develop, retain and reward quality staff who are committed to the educational goals and the mission of the University.

We must ensure that University of Jaffna is seen as a means of achieving professional success and personal growth. I will drive the University of Jaffna to support the professional development of all staff, to ensure that staff teach in ways that are efficient and effective as well as rewarding, to ensure activities are allocated appropriately to academic and professional staff, to create the time, space and facilities needed for innovative research, and to recognize and reward excellence.

University of Jaffna is expected to play a major role in the regional development. Therefore, I will drive the staff and the students to support and respond to the educational and research needs of the broader community. I will also support, and wherever appropriate, lead action to mitigate social harm from academic fraud, environmental degradation, social exclusion, and political and cultural discord. If the University community – the students, staff and alumni – can contribute to this endeavour, then together we will continue to make a real difference to the citizens of this country.

In order to continue the University of Jaffna's commitment to the public good, we must ensure that all our students are equipped to think independently, to behave ethically and in a socially and environmentally responsible manner, and that they have the capacity and desire to continue to question, challenge and learn long after they have completed their University studies.

Q. One of the major challenges that our state-own education is facing is that inability to cater the global needs. Consequently, considerable numbers of our degree holders were unable to find suitable employment. You have expressed your concern to change this. Tell us how you think we should overcome this?

A. The priority actions have been designed within the ambit of the Global Trends in Higher Education. Let me explain the context of Global Trends in Higher Education.

The impact of market forces on higher education is through employment. The private sector, considered to be the engine of growth, is the major employer. The relevance of some courses of study to the world of work and the quality of the recent graduates has been less than optimal. Their generic skills such as communication, teamwork, computer literacy and, their work ethic and mindset have been found wanting. These have many implications for quality conscious academics and administrators.

Producing a twenty first century graduate requires a shift towards Outcome-Based Education (OBE) and Student-Centered Learning (SCL). The curriculum design process should incorporate the necessary knowledge, skills, attitudes and mindset that a graduate needs into the curriculum, which is delivered using teaching and learning methods towards facilitating student centered learning. Assessment and evaluation should ensure that the graduate has achieved the intended learning outcomes. A continuous process of quality improvement has to be sustained through monitoring and feedback from employers and other stakeholders.

The impact of Science, Technology and Innovation in all aspects of life has increased globally. Achieving a better quality of life for the people in developing countries needs the collaboration of Universities with industry in generating new knowledge and, in transmitting and adapting existing knowledge to suit local needs. The demand for non-formal education is increasing. Adults who are in work wish to enhance their skills and competencies, which enhance their value in a knowledge economy. The concept of lifelong education is gaining popularity. Universities and HEIs which usually provide full time degree courses to young students directly from secondary school by the face to face mode, are now beginning to offer more extension courses to mature students, often by the open and distance mode.

There is a movement towards a 'global' benchmark in education, a standard of excellence that all could aspire to. There is a developing concept of 'World Class Universities' as centers of excellence, which all countries would aspire to have. Paradoxically this has led to a market driven expansion of Higher Education across borders, which in the absence of regulation has led to a wide variation in the quality of courses being offered and create concern for quality assurance more than ever before. Being aware of this trend is important to respond to societal needs.

Q. What are your Strategic objectives?

A. I have identified four strategic objectives. How to transform student life through learning.

The ultimate purpose of learning is character formation. I aim to provide students with a supportive and a challenging learning environment in which they can develop their academic, personal capabilities and skills, and thereby become effective, educated and ethical graduates.

I will enable the University to provide opportunities for students to develop the English language and interpersonal skills, and knowledge to operate effectively in a global environment, particularly through industrial/community study experiences and to facilitate interactions between industrial partners and communities to enhance intercultural understanding.

Second, to create new and useful knowledge. To focus on improving the University of Jaffna's international and national performance, and ranking in both fundamental and in applied research. I encourage our research effort and resources on areas of demonstrable research strength, and to cultivate new research interests. Collaboration with communities and industries will be encouraged in knowledge exchange. Focus my efforts to increase quantity and quality of research, develop knowledge exchange programmes with industry and professional partners to support development through University Business Linkage (UBL) programmes.

Third, to support and reward staff excellence. To achieve the vision of the University of Jaffna "to be a leading center of excellence in teaching, learning and scholarship." Realizing this vision requires us to attract, retain, develop, recognize and reward the best staff. Supporting our staff and ensuring their time is allocated productively and efficiently is a foundation for our teaching and research efforts. The University will need to plan for the development, growth and renewal of its workforce, and be responsive to the interests of the staff and to changing labor market conditions. Actions will be undertaken to develop and implement a transparent and equitable academic workload management system, develop and implement a strategic and well understood system for setting and reviewing accountability of performance goals for every member of staff annually.

Fourth, how to strengthen Institutional Governance. The term "governance" is used to describe all those structures, processes and activities that are involved in the planning and direction of the institutions and people working there. Good governance is critical to the effective operation of the University and to its ability to make a full contribution towards its mission. Every system is capable of further enhancement and good governance should continuously evolve. In line with the key principle of academic autonomy – I will lead the Council and the Senate of the University, as far as possible, as critical forums of discussion, debate and decision-making where academics of the university can together evolve the functioning of the university to attain the objectives detailed above.

I will do my utmost best to make sure that the interests of the university as understood and interpreted by its academic community, guide all decisions I take as their peer-leader and will not allow extraneous elements who have other extraneous goals to impede the governance of the university. Since Higher education is fundamental to the knowledge creation and the social, economic and cultural health of the nation, I will promote the values that characterize higher education: respect for evidence; respect for individuals and their views; the search for truth; and care for the wellbeing of democratic civilization.

Q. After speaking to students and staffers in the University we came to know that you have introduced best practices to strengthen the management and improve the environment for students. Tell us more.

A. In line with Institutional Review guidelines, I have ensured that the following Best practices are adopted by the University:

The University complies with the national policy framework for higher education which includes standards and guidelines issued by the MoHE, UGC and QAAC and other professional bodies where applicable, e.g. Sri Lanka Medical Council (SLMC) for Medicine. It will as far as possible also comply with other reference points such as the Sri Lanka Qualifications Framework (SLQF), Subject Benchmark Statements(SBS) and Codes of Practice.

Participatory management is promoted with a flexible mix of formal and informal mechanisms, which encourage teamwork in a transparent manner. Informal/ad-hoc committees complement the work of the statutory bodies. Monitoring and evaluation procedures are built into all departments and programmes.

Managing resources such as space, money, material and human resources form the crux of organizational management based on forecasting, planning, implementation, and monitoring. The Institution complies with national administrative and financial regulations as well its own pre-approved Manual of Procedures or Standard Operational Procedures (SOPs).

Information and Communication Technology (ICT) is integrated into the system for teaching and learning, administration, research and community engagement. A user friendly Management Information System (MIS) will be in place for effective and efficient management of operations. This system allows information to be logically stored and easily retrieved for instant availability of information and swift execution of tasks in a cost effective and efficient manner.

Administration is receptive to the welfare of staff and students and adequate welfare measures are in place for staff and students to function optimally.

The University has a clearly defined code of conduct for all categories of staff emphasizing the maintenance of the highest moral and ethical standards. This is effectively communicated to all staff at the time of appointment to the institution.

The University strives to promote Gender Equity and Equality (GEE) and deter any form of sexual and Gender-Based Violence (SGBV) amongst all categories of staff and students by adopting an appropriate policy and strategy drawn up in line with the UGC prescribed policy and strategy (on GEE and SGBV) and it is spearheaded through a task force/coordinating body with necessary empowerments and resources for effective implementation.

Q. What are your priorities and how do you expect to accomplish them during your tenure?

A. Build the physical facilities and human resources in the newly established Faculty of Technology as proposed in the project proposal.

Strengthen the Faculty of Engineering by enhancing Laboratory facilities and student numbers for obtaining the professional accreditation. Implementing the community engagement projects of the Faculty of agriculture by utilizing the facilities obtained with the funding from JICA project.

Complete the ongoing building projects of the Faculty of Management and Commerce and shift the Faculty from its temporary main premises to its new premises. Provide the necessary infrastructure and staff facilities to the Department of Law to conduct its academic programme in a conducive manner, and lay a foundation for it to become a faculty with different departments of specialization.

Initiate actions to revamp the curriculum of the Faculty of Arts to incorporate transferrable skills and interpersonal skills as sandwiched components of the curriculum to enable the Arts graduates to be readily employable. Expediting the upgrading the Ramanathan Academy of Fine Arts as Faculty/Institute with good facilities. Completing the process of building for the Department of Computer Science of the Faculty of Science with the generous funding of AHEAD project.

Take steps to establish the Faculty of Marine Sciences and Aquatic Resources Technology. Complete the building for the Professorial Unit of the Faculty of Medicine. Establish the Institute/Faculty of Siddha Medicine with improved facilities. Build more residential and recreational facilities at Ariviyal Nagar for students and staff.

Complete the ongoing infrastructure projects of the Vavuniya Campus in the Pambaimadu site and take steps to devolve the campus as a university. Complete and equip the Indoor Stadium cum Gymnasium of the University of Jaffna. Build IT center and, enhance Broadband access and IT services. Modernize Library with the state of art facilities and create more space
for it.

Q. We would like to have a brief introduction on the most recent initiative of establishing City University in which you also are playing a significant role.

A. City Universities are determined to cater the human resource needs of the identified regions (Hambantota, Kalutara, Matale, NuwaraEliya and Mullaitivu). In order to materialize the creation of such new entities, Professor Gamini Senanayake, Senior Professor in Agricultural Biology, University of Ruhuna appointed in June 2020, as the Lead Consultant for the project development of the City University in Sri Lanka by the UGC and the Ministry of Higher Education.

Professor. Gamini Senanayake has been entrusted to lead, advice and coordinate the proposal development of the establishment of initially, five City Universities in Sri Lanka. In this regard, I was appointed as the Senior Consultant and Professor B. Nimalathasan, Professor in Accounting, University of Jaffna was appointed as the Junior Consultant for the proposal development of Mullaitivu City University (MCU).

Mullaitivu was one of the hardest hit areas by the three decades of war. People suffered during the long years of this conflict, many continue to suffer its longer term impacts. Women and children with disabilities are also most vulnerable group in post-conflict situation, experiencing the highest levels of gender-related violence, abject poverty, and exclusion.

Shortage of Knowledge and Technology based human resources in Mullaitivu caused adverse effects on the society. As at present, this gap is filled mostly by the Day Scholars from Jaffna district who travels 230kms every day. It is regretted to note that no vocational or higher educational institute is located in this region for tertiary education. Mullaitivu is a vast region sharing the boundaries with Pulmoddai in Trincomalee district in the east and with Mallavi in Mannar district in the west. Mullaitivu City University (MCU) will help to address this urgent requirement.

21

MUST TAKE AN UNEQUIVOCAL STAND AGAINST ALL FORMS OF HATE

If you have fundamentalists in power, things will deteriorate very quickly, even for believers, as a believer is not the same as a fundamentalist.

~

Maryam Namazie
Iranian-born writer and activist

SHE is energetic and outspoken. Her creativity on resistance against repressive regimes has attracted many communities around the globe. Maryam Namazie is an Iranian-born writer and activist based in London. She is the Spokesperson for Fitnah – Movement for Women's Liberation, One Law for All and the Council of Ex-Muslims of Britain. She hosts a weekly television program in Persian and English called Bread and Roses. No doubt because of her activities for protecting and promoting human freedom, she is a top enemy of the country where she born.

Maryam was born in Tehran, but she left Iran with her family in 1980 after the establishment of the Islamic Republic. She then lived in India, the UK and then settled in the US where she began her university studies at the age of 17. After graduating, Maryam went to Sudan to work with Ethiopian refugees. Halfway through her stay, an Islamic government took power. She was threatened by the government for establishing a clandestine human rights organisation and had to be evacuated by her employer for her own safety.

Back in the United States, Maryam worked for various refugee and human rights organisations. She established the Committee for Humanitarian Assistance to Iranian Refugees in 1991. In 1994, she went to Turkey and produced a video documentary on the situation of Iranian refugees there.

The Islamic regime of Iran's media outlets has called Maryam 'immoral and corrupt' and did an 'exposé' on her entitled 'Meet this anti-religion woman'. In 2019, the Islamic regime's intelligence service did a TV program where Maryam was featured as "anti-God".

"No religion promotes an inclusive society. Religion is an exclusive club that sees its set of beliefs as superior to other sets of beliefs," she said. "Inequality is a pillar of Sharia courts but this is not just the case for Sharia courts," she added.

In this interview I have communicated with her on life in Iran, consequences of Sharia and religious courts, Easter Sunday's bombings in Sri Lanka, and her readings on terrorism and radicalisation.

Following are excerpts from the interview:
Q: Thank you for joining us Maryam! Tell us what is One Law for All initiative all about? And why is it important to have such an initiative?

One Law for All was established to oppose Sharia and religious courts because they are inhuman and abuse human rights. This is the case whether the courts are in Iran and Saudi Arabia or in Britain. One's religion or belief is a basic right and a private matter.
Religious courts, however, have nothing to do with the right to religion and are part of the Islamist project to control and manage women, minorities and dissenters. We know Sharia's criminal code includes the death penalty for apostasy and blasphemy and stoning to death for gay sex or sex outside of marriage. It is unbelievably brutal.

In Britain, Sharia courts deal mainly with the family code, which some feel is trivial but the code is highly discriminatory against women and legitimises violence against women. For example, under Sharia's family code, a woman's testimony is worth half of a man's, marital rape is not seen as a crime and child marriage and polygamy are deemed acceptable. One Law for All argues minority women from Muslim backgrounds should have the same rights in the family as other citizens.

Inequality is a pillar of Sharia courts but this is not just the case for Sharia courts. The Jewish Beth Din in the UK, for example, also puts women in limbo by refusing to grant them divorces without their husband's permission. We know also historically about the role played by ecclesiastic courts. One Law for All argues that it is dangerous to put the rights of citizens in the hands of mullahs, priests and rabbis. Secular states, public policy and laws are the best way to ensure the rights of all citizens irrespective of background and belief.

Q: You were born in Iran and then moved to other places. Tell us about your childhood and the life in Iran till you left your motherland?

My parents are secular Muslims so I never had any religion imposed on me at home and never felt lesser for being a girl. In fact, I have always felt supported and loved even after I became an atheist.

I never really felt religion's influence on my life until the Islamists took power in Iran.

Then things changed dramatically. There were Islamists sent to my school to separate the boys from the girls in the playground, executions on TV and the beginnings of compulsory veiling and the rest is as they say unfolding history. After living under an Islamic state, I realised very quickly though that religion in the state is heinous and why I campaign against it.

Prior to it, Iran was under the Shah's dictatorship and for a time, the revolution gave everyone hope for real change but the Islamists took hold of it, slaughtered a generation and 40 years on, people have been living in a theocracy in the 21st century.

Q: What went wrong in Iran?

If you have fundamentalists in power, things will deteriorate very quickly, even for believers, as a believer is not the same as a fundamentalist. This isn't a theoretical discussion. We can see the effects of a theocracy on the lives of freethinkers, women, LGBT, religious minorities and especially young people in countries like Iran or Saudi Arabia but we can also see what happens when even secular societies are run by theocrats.

Look at Modi's India where Muslims can be killed for eating beef. Look at the situation for abortion rights, for example, in the US with the rise of the Christian-Right. Or the situation of Muslims in Myanmar and so on. In Sri Lanka, too, you have extremist Sinhala Buddhist groups like Bodu Bala Sena which have had a detrimental effect on religious and other minorities and women.

This is the problem with identity politics everywhere. It reduces masses of people to just one religious or cultural identity though people are much more complex than that and have countless characteristics that define them. Identity politics reduces 21st-century citizens into warring tribes.

Which is why after the horrendous Easter Sunday terrorist attack in Sri Lanka, ordinary Muslims going about their lives are collectively blamed and we see Muslims being run out of their homes (including some ex-Muslims I know in Sri Lanka) or Muslim shops are burnt down. Also, refugees from Pakistan who have fled to Sri Lanka because of Islamist persecution become displaced again when they are run out of their homes. How can terrorising innocent people be a solution for terrorist attacks against other innocent people?

Q: Some of the reports indicated that you are ex-Muslim. Is that true?

I am an ex-Muslim and work with ex-Muslims in Sri Lanka and elsewhere too. Of course, our atheism is our private affair, it's a matter of conscience and belief, but when people can be killed for apostasy and blasphemy, we feel the need to say we are ex-Muslims publicly to challenge the status quo and defend the right to expression and conscience without fear of persecution or discrimination.

Q: Why are you against Sharia Law?

As I mentioned, all religious laws are discriminatory. The problem with Sharia and other religious laws is that they are coercive.

If religion is a personal belief, then why do you need laws to enforce it? For example, some Muslims in my family fast during Ramadan and others have never fasted. This is the personal choice of adults.

However, in Iran or Saudi Arabia because of Sharia law, one will be flogged or imprisoned for eating during Ramadan. Examples abound such as in the case of compulsory veiling. If an adult doesn't want to wear the veil, why do you need morality police to beat a woman, arrest her? Or if someone doesn't believe in Islam, well that is their freedom of conscience.

Why must the state execute someone for atheism? Religious law is fundamentally unjust as it forces people to do not what they believe but that which the mullahs and clerics in power tell them. Coercion and violence go hand in hand with Sharia courts.

Q: Sri Lanka is the latest victim of self-proclaimed Islamic State. What is your reading on the attacks in Sri Lanka?

We at Council of Ex-Muslims of Britain along with other atheist groups (including the Council of Ex-Muslims of Sri Lanka) expressed our outrage at the terrorist attacks and also mourned the many killed.

In our statement, we said:

"We are outraged at the Islamist attacks on churches and hotels in Sri Lanka. Our hearts go out to the survivors and victims – hundreds killed, including at least 45 children, and more than 500 wounded. We mourn them with the people of Sri Lanka and the world.

"The terrorists claim to have killed innocent Christians and others in order to 'avenge' innocent Muslims killed in Christchurch; the Christchurch terrorist also feigned to kill innocent Muslim worshippers as an act of 'vengeance'. What should by now be very clear to everyone is that these terrorist attacks have nothing to do with addressing grievances – real or imagined – and everything to do with using terror, hate, supremacy and violence as a tool to impose the ideology and dominance of the religious-Right.

"Whether Islamist or white nationalist, whether in Sri Lanka or Christchurch, these far-Right movements have no respect for human life and rights: Christian, Muslim, ex-Muslim, believer or non, white, black or brown, young or old; no amount of murder or mayhem is too heinous for their hateful cause. Always anti-those deemed 'other'; always relying on hate, religion, violence, misogyny, homophobia, tribalism, xenophobia, anti-Semitism and terrorism to sow fear and division.

"For too long and still far too many continue to excuse one side over the other depending on where they stand. Some will defend the Islamists, others will defend the Christian-Right, both sides saying there are 'legitimate grievances' even if they claim to abhor terrorism. Many will even go so far as to blame the victims, especially in the case of apostates and blasphemers like Charlie Hebdo or the Bangladeshi bloggers. What these apologists fail to see is that there is no legitimisation for murder. "Those killed in Sri Lanka could be any of us. We could be next. We must all take an unequivocal stand against all forms of fascism and hate. We must not allow the conflation of the religious-Right with ordinary believers, victim blaming, and the dehumanisation of the 'other' to legitimate a politics of terror and hate. "Sooner than later, we must recognise that we are all in this together against the far-Right and in defence of our common humanity. Our lives and our rights are interlinked irrespective of our backgrounds and beliefs.

"It is a matter of urgency that governments stop appeasing theocracies and the religious-Right, including via faith schools and child indoctrination, religious courts and faith-based policies. This only strengthens divisions and the religious-Right.

"Defending secularism, citizenship and universal rights is the only way forward."

IS has killed Yazidis, Kurds, Syrians, Christians, Muslims, ex-Muslims, Atheists, young and old, women and men… From IS, Taliban, the Islamic regime in Iran to Boko Haram and Al Shabaab, no one is safe. From London to Madrid to NY to Colombo and Kabul no one feels safe. The whole point of terrorism is to target innocent civilians indiscriminately to instil hate and despair and fear. That is why courage and hope and love are so important for all of us. They want to divide us; we must insist on our common humanity.

Q: What are your suggestions and recommendations to prevent the IS' influences?

It is important that we treat everyone equally as citizens and not members of some religious or cultural 'group'. That will help focus on terrorists and criminals rather than placing collective blame on everyone who is Muslim, for example. Islamism is a political far-Right movement like the white supremacists in the US. You cannot weed out white supremacist terrorists in the US by collectively blaming all Christians or all white people. It is a political movement; you need to target it politically and also ideologically.

Also, an insistence on secularism is key. Separation of religion from the state – any religion – is crucial to bringing about lasting change. We shouldn't have religious schools, religious indoctrination in schools, religion in the law or public policy or in the state's dealings with citizens.

Also, I think we need to look at rights from a universalist perspective – we all have inalienable rights no matter what our background. And most importantly, we all share a common humanity. We are in this together – Muslim, ex-Muslim, Buddhist, Jew, Christian, atheist… - against the fundamentalists and fascists of all stripes who kill with impunity and have no regard for human rights or lives.

Q: Would you say Islam does not promote an inclusive society?

 No religion promotes an inclusive society. Religion is an exclusive club that sees its set of beliefs as superior to other sets of beliefs. In any religion, the apostates, heretics, witches and blasphemers within the religion are imprisoned and killed. Those who are not part of the religion are seen to be lesser.

To include citizens in a society, you must exclude religion to some extent from the public space. People, of course, have a right to religion and belief but it cannot be part of the state or law or public policy or the educational system if we want to ensure that religion has its rightful place in our societies and world – as a personal matter.

Q: What is your message to those who undermined and side-lined your basic rights when you were under repressive governments, as we as to those who joined and planning to join the terrorist outfit like Islamic State?

My message to those who join IS or other terrorist groups and repressive governments are the same: we will never bow down. There are many more of us than there are of you. Also, hate can never kill love and hope and that is our strongest weapon against the fundamentalists of all stripes.

22

TRUTH BEHIND THE EASTER MASSACRE IN SRI LANKA

It appears that ISIS didn't choose Sri Lanka, but that a group Sri Lankans chose ISIS.

~

Jonah Blank
Principal Investigator and Senior Political Scientist for RAND Corporation

SRI LANKA is passing through one of most sensitive periods of its history in the aftermath of brutal assault on the nation targeting the country's churches and luxury hotels by a group of terrorists on Easter Sunday. In this interview I have communicated with Jonah Blank, a Principal Investigator and Senior Political Scientist for RAND Corporation, to understand his points of view on the prevailing situation in the country as well as jihad movements.

RAND was established almost 70 years ago to strengthen public policy through research and analysis. According to the available history on RAND, "On 14 May 1948, Project RAND—an organisation formed immediately after World War II to connect military planning with research and development decisions—separated from the Douglas Aircraft Company of Santa Monica, California, and became an independent, non-profit organisation." Significantly, on the same day the State of Israel was declared by David Ben-Gurion. RAND, as the one of the top research centres consisted of over 1,900 staff and maintained in locations spreading across 50 countries, 'has continuously demonstrated that rigorous research and analysis can help address some of the world's most challenging problems'.

Graduated from Harvard, he has taught anthropology and politics at Harvard, Georgetown, and George Washington University's Elliot School for International Affairs. Since 2003, he has been a Professorial Lecturer at Johns Hopkins School of Advanced International Studies (SAIS). Before joining the RAND, Jonah Blank served as Policy Director for South and Southeast Asia on the staff of the Senate Foreign Relations Committee in the United States of America. At various times, his Senate portfolio also included Africa, the Middle East, and Central Asia.

In this interview, Jonah observes two significant issues on the Easter Sunday bombings in Sri Lanka. First, the attack was a result of the political negligence than its accounting as an intelligence failure by many parties. Second, Islamic State of Iraq and Syria (ISIS) didn't choose Sri Lanka, but the Sri Lankan extremists chose ISIS.

Meanwhile, suggesting how to solve the political crisis in the country, he says: "When the nation's two top officials are locked in open conflict, they can't cooperate to ensure the safety of the citizens."

Following are excerpts:

Q: Jonah, thank you for joining us. First of all, let our readers know about you; your academic background, present engagements and so on?

A: I'm a senior political scientist at the RAND Corporation, focusing on South and Southeast Asia. I'm an anthropologist by training, currently based in Indonesia. I am the author of two books: 'Arrow of the Blue-Skinned God,' which retraces the epic 'Ramayana' through India and Sri Lanka, and 'Mullahs on the Mainframe,' which explores Islam and modernity.

Q: Currently you are based in Jakarta, Indonesia, a country suffering mainly from two enemies – first, natural disaster and second, jihad extremism. Therefore, Indonesia's long-prevailing moderate Islam is slowly but surely crumbling and shattering as fundamentalists seize the popular movements, though movements such as Indonesia's Nahdlatul Ulama oppose Wahhabism. We would like to know your findings?

A: I think this overstates the issue: Islam in Indonesia is indeed changing and becoming more globalised—but that's true for Islam (and all religions) everywhere. Violent Islamist groups were far more active in Indonesia in the half-decade after the fall of Suharto than they are now; the main local terrorist group, Jemaah Islamiyah, has essentially been disbanded (or, at least, it's just a shadow of its former self). This is not to say that extremism is itself gone – merely that its terrorist fringe is more controlled now than it was 15 years ago.

Q: Let's talk about Sri Lanka. What is your view on the recent suicide attacks by a so-called local branch of the self-identified Islamic State (IS/ISIS) in Sri Lanka?

A: This set of attacks is unimaginably tragic – and utterly unexpected. Sri Lanka has endured a horrific civil war, and a huge amount of terrorism associated with it, but it had never before seen this type of action. That is, the terrorism it had experienced in the past was almost entirely based on politics and ethnic identity, not on religion. Christians had never before been targeted for their faith, and global terrorist groups like ISIS had never been active.

Q: Why do they choose Sri Lanka?

A: It appears that ISIS didn't choose Sri Lanka, but that a group Sri Lankans chose ISIS. It could have happened anywhere, but in this case the terrorists happened to be Sri Lankan, and they got their skill-set and training (apparently) from ISIS.

Q: Do you think the ISIS' lone wolf strategy was used in this attack?

A: No, this was the opposite of a 'lone wolf' attack: A lone wolf attack is typically when an individual (not a group) simply plans and executes an attack with no external support from ISIS apart from ideological inspiration. Usually, this is something very simple: Driving a car into a crowd, or opening fire with firearms. The Sri Lanka attacks were the opposite of this: They were very carefully planned and executed, most likely with external assistance from ISIS.

Q: What are the differences between the armed rebellions led by the LTTE ended in 2009 and the prevailing threat of jihad extremism in Sri Lanka?

A: The two are not linked. The LTTE occasionally targeted Muslims, but it did so for political rather than ideological reasons (i.e., when Muslim groups refused to advance LTTE aims). In terms of impact, the LTTE was (until 2009) a far greater threat to Sri Lanka than any Islamist group might be. But the Easter attacks do show just how much damage a small group of dedicated terrorists can cause.

Q: Many argued that a gross intelligence failure led to the success of the attacks. But if we go back in history, we can see many intelligence agencies' warnings going unheard. What do you think?

A: It's always easy to second-guess after the fact. But in this case it does appear as if there was a political failure which led to a poor Government response. The warnings from an external intelligence agency (almost certainly India) were reportedly relayed to the office of President Sirisena. It seems as if these warnings were not acted on sufficiently – and were not relayed to Prime Minister Wickremesinghe. There are two reasons for this: First, the President does not trust the Prime Minister (he tried to have him ousted in October 2018), and there is bad blood between them. Second, the President believes that India favours the Prime Minister over him, so he may have discounted the intelligence on these grounds.

Q: There are some reports suggesting that foreign intelligence agencies did not share the important details about Sri Lankan youth who were motivated by radical thoughts during their higher studies abroad. What do you suggest?

A: There is so much raw intelligence floating around that it would be foolish to assume any particular pieces of it might have unlocked the puzzle. Yes, there was genuine and important intelligence out there – but how is one to find it in the mass of incorrect information also floating around?

Q: Do you have any suggestions to prevent such attacks in the future?

A: A few suggestions, for Sri Lanka:

1. End the political stalemate between the President and Prime Minister: When the nation's two top officials are locked in open conflict, they can't cooperate to ensure the safety of the citizens. If necessary, hold new elections — or just find a way of working together better.

2. Cooperate with other nations on intelligence-sharing regarding counterterrorism. India's intelligence was not acted on, this time, and India has a lot of information to offer. The US, Britain and other nations do as well.

3. Work with the Sri Lankan Muslim communities. Sri Lanka's previous record on counterterrorism and counterinsurgency isn't good: The Government alienated the Tamil population through brutal actions, which served to increase support for the LTTE and strengthen this insurgent/terrorist group. The Government should not make the same mistake with its Muslim populations.

Q: Some intelligent and well-read youth are fighting for IS and turning into human bombs, leaving their lavish lifestyles. What is your reading on this social phenomenon as an anthropologist?

A: It is now widely accepted within academic and policy circles that economic deprivation is not the primary driver of terrorism: It's quite common for terrorists (including suicide bombers) to be relatively well-educated and at least middle or lower-middle class. It is unusual for them to be wealthy, but Osama bin Laden was a billionaire.

Q: In addition to other countries, the United States too is being blamed for causing the mushrooming of the jihad terror groups. Do you think US foreign policy and its strategies need to be restructured?

A: I think there are many aspects of US foreign policy that could benefit from considerable reformulation.

Q: Thank you for your time and valuable thoughts, Jonah. Hope to talk to you again. One last query here. Please share with us your message to the general public, policymakers, and members of the law enforcement agencies in Sri Lanka on curbing radicalised minds and eliminating jihad terrorism?

A: Thank you for asking me. The best way to combat terrorism (in Sri Lanka and elsewhere) is through careful intelligence sharing/gathering and close cooperation with the communities in which terrorists recruit. The Sri Lanka bombers, after all, had already been shunned by the local Muslim communities they'd come from. If the Government had been cooperating better with its own Muslim citizens, it might have known about these individuals before it was too late.

23

EASTER SUNDAY ATTACK WAS IDEOLOGICAL

The Islamic State as a US creation is total nonsense. Such a claim is misinformation or classical Freudian projection, accusing others of what you yourself are doing.

~

Lawrence Sellin
Retired US Army Reserve Colonel

THE EASTER Sunday terror attack in Sri Lanka marked a dark chapter in the nation's history, as over 250 innocent lives were brutally taken in a coordinated assault, leaving hundreds more with life-altering injuries. This devastating event, the most sophisticated of its kind in Sri Lanka, introduced the country to the grim reality of Islamist terrorism. The Islamic State claimed responsibility for the heinous crimes, shattering the peace that the island nation had long enjoyed. Both local and foreign intelligence agencies had issued warnings about potential attacks by extremists, highlighting the growing global threat of Islamist extremism.

In an interview, Lawrence Sellin, a retired US Army Reserve Colonel with extensive experience in Special Forces, Infantry, Chemical, and Medical Services, shared his insights on the prevailing threats posed by extremists and the specifics of the Easter Sunday attack. Colonel Sellin, having served in conflict zones like Afghanistan and Iraq, brought a wealth of knowledge to the discussion. His diverse background included participation in humanitarian missions to West Africa, showcasing the multifaceted challenges faced by nations dealing with extremism on a global scale.

Colonel Sellin's expertise extended beyond his military service, as evidenced by his Master's Degree in Strategic Studies from the US Army War College. Fluent in Arabic, Kurdish, and French, he received language training at the Defence Language Institute, underscoring the importance of linguistic proficiency in navigating complex geopolitical landscapes. Following his military career, Sellin transitioned into a distinguished civilian path, excelling in medical research and international business, earning a Ph.D. in physiology along the way. His interview provided valuable insights into the multifaceted dimensions of the Easter Sunday attack and the broader challenges posed by terrorism in the contemporary world.

Following are excerpts:

Q: Col. Sellin, thank you for joining us. I believe this is the very first interview you are giving to the Sri Lankan press. Could you tell us about yourself and your service as one of the senior military officers deployed in Middle East?

A: Yes, this is my first interview with the Sri Lankan press. I served 29 years as an officer in the US Army Reserve. Unlike active duty personnel, reservists have parallel civilian careers, which, in my case, was in the international information technology business after approximately 15 years in medical research for which I obtained a Ph.D. in physiology. I am a graduate of the US Army Special Warfare School, commonly known as the Green Berets, and I have branch qualifications and assignment experience in Infantry, Chemical and the Medical Services Corps. I served two tours in Afghanistan, the first as an embedded trainer with the Afghan Army, which took me all along the Afghan-Pakistan border from Nuristan to Helmand Provinces. For the second tour, I was a staff officer at the International Security Assistance Force (ISAF) Headquarters in Kabul.

I was deployed to northern Iraq in 2008-2009, where I was involved efforts to improve counterinsurgency command and control and defensive measures against, for example, attacks using anti-armour grenades (RKG-3) and various types of improvised explosive devices whether fixed or vehicle-borne.

I was also responsible for the humanitarian component of a special operations mission to West Africa in 2007, where we delivered medical, dental and veterinary services to rural villages.

Q: You are a member of the Citizens Commission of National Security. Could you tell us about the role of this initiative?

A: The Citizens Commission on National Security is one group of which I am a member. It is composed of individuals with experience in the military, intelligence, diplomacy, legislation, and the media to exert an impact on the strength and security of America by holding both politicians and the media accountable for policy formulation and accurate reporting.

Q: Do you think US foreign policy on Middle East and elsewhere did not address the root causes of the problems but caused towards further worsening?

A: Like all countries, the US has had both successes and failures in foreign policy. The root causes of problems are not always obvious at the time a decision is required, they vary by local conditions and they often evolve over time. It is, therefore, only in retrospect can we most effectively analyse and learn from both successes and failures in national policies. In some cases, I think US involvement improved the situation, in some cases not.

Q: What are the positive achievements of the US's military interventions in Middle East?

A: Because it is too early in a strategic sense to evaluate them, I would not describe them as achievements, but certain courses of actions, I think, were necessary, like the defeat of the Islamic State in Syria and Iraq.

On the other hand, I think there has been too much eagerness on the part of recent US administrations to intervene when it shouldn't or to intervene appropriately, but then employ strategies that proved counterproductive. Obama's Arab Spring policies were a total disaster. The removal of Saddam Hussein was beneficial to the Iraqi people, but the invasion and the methods implemented subsequently ended up destabilising and disrupting a balance of power in the region, unnecessarily benefiting Iran. Although the 2001 removal of the Taliban regime in Afghanistan was the correct course of action, the counterinsurgency and nation-building approach did not address the problems created by Pakistan, which has ultimately led to a failure after an initial success.

Q: Islamist extremist groups are mushrooming around the globe. Their latest testing ground is South Asia. Why is the US and its alliance unable to vanquish this problem, though adequate resources have been allocated to implement the strategies?

A: Although based on the select interpretation of religious tenets, Islamist extremism is an international problem not substantially different from other totalitarian threats such as fascism or communism. At this stage, Islamists use the techniques of subversion i.e. radicalisation, infiltration of target societies and anarchist-like violence to achieve its aims of a global caliphate and the implementation of sharia.

The instigators of that extremism and operating continuously in the background are the global promoters of austere and often intolerant forms of Islam such as Wahhabism-Salafism, financed either by wealthy individuals or nation-states that offer forums for radicalisation and sources for potential jihadi recruits.

Al Qaeda and the Islamic State, for example, are brands or franchises more than specific entities, who exploit local and regional grievances or power vacuums and provide the operational arm for radicalised jihadis in terms of terrorist training and support. Combating the terrorist network requires a coordinated international effort addressing the radicalisation process, stopping the international financing, often involving the narcotics trade, and, in particular, sanctioning the nation states acting as facilitators.

Q: Some reports have been published saying that the USA is funding the Islamist extremists. In fact, the Islamic State of Iraq and Syria known ISIS is nothing but their creation. What do you think?

A: The Islamic State as a US creation is total nonsense. Such a claim is misinformation or classical Freudian projection, accusing others of what you yourself are doing. There are, however, cases where the US badly misjudged the groups it supported, a good example being Obama's disastrous Arab Spring policy and the US interventions associated with it.

Q: You were highly critical about Pakistan. In many of your writings, you have pointed that Pakistan, especially its state spy agency known as Inter-Service Intelligence (ISI), is sponsoring the Islamist extremists. However, the US has a long history of maintaining a goodwill relationship with Pakistan. Don't you think the US has the responsibility for course correction in Pakistan?

A: The Trump Administration may have turned the corner on US relations with Pakistan, finally recognising Pakistan's duplicity regarding its relationship with the US in the Afghanistan war. While accepting US aid, Pakistan has been conducting a proxy war against Afghanistan and the US through its support of the Taliban. Pakistan is an ally of China and its aims in Afghanistan have never coincided with those of the US I believe we will see a further US alignment with India and an increased US propensity to support sanctions against Pakistan for its facilitation of Islamist extremism. In all those respects, Pakistan has chosen to make itself an enemy of the US.

Q: In your recent article about Jihad's infiltration to South Asia, you have discussed Easter Sunday bombings in Sri Lanka. That was paradigm shift in the island nation. Do you think Sri Lanka's war on drugs caused this move of Islamist extremists who are getting large funds out of selling drugs?

A: There is no doubt that Islamist extremists use drug trafficking and other criminal activities to support their violent operations.

It is a means to an end. The Easter Sunday attack was ideological, not a response to Sri Lanka's actions to prevent illicit drug sales. If anything, the bombings should motivate the Sri Lankan authorities to undertake greater efforts to block that source of terrorist financing.

Q: Many conspiracy theories are popping up over the Easter Sunday bombings in Sri Lanka. Some of them are arguing it is an act of Saudi Arabia with the help of US intelligence agency to dismantle the Chinese involvement in the island nation. In fact, a leaked alleged classified letter by the Saudi Arabian Foreign Ministry to its Embassy in Colombo warned of such attack days ahead. How do you look at them as a military veteran who fought some of the most difficult wars in the century?

A: I think Sri Lanka is aware and increasingly wary of China's debt-trap diplomacy. Of course, the US does not wish Sri Lanka to become overly dependent upon or obligated to China. Any concerns that the US may harbour, however, could be easily resolved through normal discourse within the context of the decades of friendly relations between the US and Sri Lanka.

It is truly absurd and delusional to believe that the US would involve itself or even be privy to such a heinous crime that took place in Sri Lanka on Easter Sunday. Serious suggestions of that nature can only originate from a deliberate disinformation campaign. There are now widely published reports that India provided warnings several times starting weeks before the attack. It is said that alerts came from the Sri Lankan Muslim community itself and alarm bells should have been set off by the January seizure of explosives by Sri Lankan security forces. It is possible that Saudi Arabia might have suspected a possible attack given the connections between the bombers and a variety of Saudi-funded Wahhabi/Salafist organisations and feedback obtained from them. But it all remains speculation at this point.

Q: Sri Lanka is fresh ground for ISIS terrorism, though extremist thoughts started spreading in the island since the mid-'80s. What is your advice to the people in the governing system and law enforcement agencies in Sri Lanka on conquering this new threat?

A: Primarily, I recommend heightened national vigilance, maintaining contact with responsible members of the Sri Lankan Muslim community and close cooperation with international partners dedicated to the reduction of Islamist extremism. Radicalisation is the first step in the recruitment of violent jihadis, where the monitoring of social media has an important preventative function as well as the adjudication of local grievances. International connections and the movement of suspects involving terrorist financing, training or links to the intelligence services of facilitating nation-states are of equal importance.

24

HOW TO READ THE NEWSPAPER?

When you are reading the newspaper, don't forget to have a pinch of salt at your side. Maintain a healthy dose of skepticism in your perspective.

~

Nury Vittachi
journalist and author

HE is a known man in Hong Kong SAR. Nury Vittachi is a journalist and author based in Hong Kong. Known as "Mister Jam" among his readers, Nury is one of the most widely published Asian writers. He has written more than 30 books, ranging from non-fiction works to novels to stories for children. His newspaper columns are syndicated daily throughout Asia. An award-winning journalist, he has had regular slots on the BBC, CNN, as well as having held senior editorial positions at the Far Eastern Economic Review and the South China Morning Post.

In this interview I have communicated with Nury on several issues such as the situation in Hong Kong and his memories about late Tarzie Vittachi.

Following are the excerpts of the interview:

Q: Nury, when was the last time you were in Sri Lanka?

A: I miss Sri Lanka so much! I haven't been for at least seven or eight years. But I keep in touch with friends and family there, so am always interested in the lively happenings of that wonderful community (and perhaps less wonderful politicians!).

Q: How is life in Hong Kong, what do you do there?

A: Life in Hong Kong is good. The economy is strong, the Government is efficient, and the press is free. The Western media constantly prints articles about the loss of press freedom here, but they are not true. I write books and articles all the time, and I am regularly rude to the leader of Hong Kong and the leader of China. I have had no trouble getting my columns and books in print.

Q: Hong Kong is a special administrative region under the People's Republic of China since 1997. What are differences you see between Mainland China and Hong Kong SAR?

A: They are both developing in interesting ways – both are becoming freer in some ways. In Hong Kong, you can say anything you like and print books saying anything. In China, you are more aware of certain limits, but people are smart – they talk about other things and often get around restrictions using clever language. The Chinese Government has pulled 850 million people out of poverty since the 1980s – this is an extraordinary achievement that it does not get enough credit for. Both governments are fundamentally good.

Q: What made you base yourself in Hong Kong?

A: I came here on honeymoon in 1987. My wife and I loved it, and so extended our honeymoon. It has lasted 32 years so far – must be one of the longest honeymoons on record.

Q: What can Sri Lanka learn from Hong Kong?

A: That's a tricky question, because Hong Kong thrived as a very benign dictatorship. (Singapore thrived as a semi-benign dictatorship.) Yet no one would recommend that any community moves away from democracy towards dictatorship – that would be insane.

But somewhere there is a sweet spot. A community needs a good, strong, wise leader, who is powerful enough to stamp out corruption—and yet gentle enough to be guided by the hopes and fears of the common people. The Judeo-Christian idea of the Servant Leader is helpful here.

I hope Sri Lanka's current or next generation will produce people like this.

Q: One of your notable works is 'The Feng Shui Detective'. What motivated you to write this book and what are the notable responses?

A: This book series was popular around the world, I am happy to say. It is a set of crime stories, but it is also a light hearted plea for people to understand each other. One of the main characters is a young female vegetarian. The other is an old Asian man who likes to eat things alive if possible! They discover that they can solve crimes only if they work together.

Q: Newspaper reports say that pro-democracy activists in Hong Kong are in danger. What is your take?

A: The Hong Kong Police are actually very good. The things you see on the internet in which they bash up protestors – these are segments from long running fights which have been edited to make it look like the police are attacking. The truth is that they are defending. But sometimes they are pushed to the limit and lose their cool. So I would say that some protestors have been violent and some police have been violent. But in the main, both have behaved quite well.

Q: Let us talk about Tarzie Vittachi, your late father and one of the best writers Ceylon ever produced. What was your earliest memory with him as a kid?

A: He was a big personality, often cheeky and rude to people, and he loved to stir things up. For example, he would say things in favour of China when people were very scared of China. But I can't honestly say he was a great father. He would disappear from the house for weeks or months on end. As a child, I saw him a strange uncle who would suddenly appear and fill the house with noise and people—and then vanish again! But he had a good heart.

Q: Many people in the country and elsewhere say that the quality of the newspapers and other media has dropped. Do you agree?

A: I can't comment on Sri Lankan newspapers, but the international press has really fallen in quality. For example, there was a march in Hong Kong which the organisers claimed involved two million people. We all knew that the organisers invented these numbers and that they would not survive even 10 minutes of fact-checking. If two million people out of a population of 7.4 million stopped work, the whole place would grind to a halt. But none of the members of the international media did the necessary fact-checking – they just printed the number that was obviously invented. Now, that "lie" has become "truth" – printed in a thousand newspapers around the world.

Q: What is the best lesson you have learnt from your father?

A: If people are sending you hate mail or angry comments, you are probably doing a good job! Shrug them off and carry on.

Q: Your father is a Ramon Magsaysay Award-winning journalist and he was the youngest Editor of the oldest newspaper in Asia, 'The Ceylon Observer,' which was founded in 1834. But, why don't we have any memoir or adequate literature about him?

A: That's a good point. A few people have started to write memoirs or biographies about him, but it seems like none have been finished. I know my mother was very much against having this sort of book written – she felt that hagiographies had no purpose, but warts-and-all biographies dug up too many negative things. But perhaps one day such a book should be written. My sister was close to him, and writes very well. Perhaps she could do it!

Q: Later, he joined the UN system. How do you observe his duties in the UNICEF?

A: He fitted in surprisingly well. Because of his big mouth, we thought he would struggle to fit into the straitjacket of that type of formal organisation. But he behaved himself for the most part, reserving his outspoken comments for the right times and the right places.

Q: Do you think journalists nowadays are less responsible?

A: Unfortunately, yes. In the old days, there was money pouring into journalism from advertisers, so we could take time to do good stories. Now the budgets are cut, reporters are few and horribly overworked, and we cut corners. It's a shame.

Q: Why is Sri Lanka still poor; what went wrong here?

A: This frustrates me so much. I know that the community is extremely smart, well-read, highly literate, and hard-working—but somehow it doesn't come together to form a thriving community that develops quickly.

We need good leaders, as I mentioned above. For most of human civilisation, humanity has been dominated by strong rulers with a measure of democracy. So for example the Greeks are said to have invented democracy, but they really pushed a model that featured rule by a wise elite, but with ways of taking into account the views of the ordinary people.

Only relatively recently have we had the model of Western liberal democracy, which takes the Greek model and moves it almost to a level of referendums, in which every person has an equal vote. Now our communities are over-politicised, which seems to be not a good thing.

I hope Sri Lanka will one day get leaders who are strong enough and honest enough and smart enough to destroy corruption and make the economy work, while still being open and inclusive enough to care for the needs of the poor and needy. That's all that's needed.

Q: Give us your advice to the writers and journalists?

A: It seems bleak, but the statistics are on our side. Asia makes up 60.5% of the world's population, yet almost none of the internationally successful books, newspapers, movies, games and other cultural items are from Asia. It is an anomaly and anomalies eventually fix themselves. So Asian writers will have to rise and take their places in the global cultural map.

Q: Late Tarzie Vittachi used to conduct lectures on how to read the newspapers. If I may ask you the same question, how to read the newspapers?

A: How to read the newspaper? Have a pinch of salt at your side. Have a little healthy scepticism in your eyes. And don't forget to read the lines and then read between the lines!

25

A JOURNEY THROUGH
MEMORIES AND PERSPECTIVES

Reconciliation is not an easy task. Many people do not follow it.

~

Selvarasa Pathmanathan
Founder, North-East Rehabilitation and Development
Organization

THE STORY of a man who transformed his life to shelter and educate hundreds of kids affected during armed conflict and due to social disparity in Sri Lanka. He is widely known as KP. Selvarasa Pathmanathan is now a social activist and founded the North-East Rehabilitation and Development Organization

When the world's one-time most wanted man is given the chance to speak, what does he say? When he is given the chance to walk freely, where does he go? When he is given time and freedom, what does he do?

His name is Selvarasa Pathmanathan, but most people refer to him as a terrorist. Known as KP, he was a driving force behind the most ruthless terrorist outfit in the world, the LTTE. Where is KP today and what has he been doing during the last decade since the brutal conflict ended in 2009?

In the second week of April in 2021, I visited Kilinochchi in the Northern Province and sat with a man, who today weighs his words more than he ever did. His life depends on his work and words more than ever before.

He is a case study in searching for the true meaning of reconciliation. He has shown that reconciliation is not merely a game of rhetoric at international forums to gain personal desires but commitments toward helping society uplift livelihoods of ordinary men and women.

Following are excerpts from the interview:

Q: Tell me about Sencholai?

A: Thank you for visiting me and for your organisation to give us some publicity. I have to thank the President for giving me this opportunity to start Sencholai. While I was in custody in Colombo, I made a request to the President, who was at the time the Defence Secretary; I told him I wanted to do something useful for the rest of my life, particularly for children and elders. He gave me permission and allowed me to visit Kilinochchi and to select a place and start a children's home. It was in 2010.

We started Anbu Children's Home in Mullaitivu then Bharathi Children's Home in the same area. These lands were previously occupied by the Army and when we requested these lands they handed it back to us. Over 100 girls who were affected by the war were enrolled and we are successfully running the school. Most of them are without parents, others with single parents. They lived a very difficult post-conflict life. We wanted to support them through their education. At the beginning in Anbu we had 30, within six months we had over 100 children. And then we started Bharathi. There are over 100 girls there. We are very successfully running this orphanage. This one we opened in 2013.

When I was arrested I thought that they were going to deport me. When I landed here, I thought to myself that my life was over. When I heard of the Defence Secretary who is the President today, I conjured up the image that he was a very serious, stern and tough person. When I landed here I thought they would take me to the cemetery. I said bye to my family in my heart and thought to myself that this life had ended, that maybe in the next life I could meet them again.

They took me to the Defence Secretary's house. When I entered I noticed in the entrance a statue of the Buddha. When I saw the light I got a feeling that I was safe. I was feeling very low at the time but when I saw this light, I felt a little energised. I sat down with the Defence Secretary and he came and shook hands with me. When he sat down and began to talk, I was thinking to myself, 'What is going on? This cannot be happening to me. This is the opposite of what should be happening to me.'

He was seated so freely and talking casually, contrary to the picture people painted and propagated of him. I got the belief that I was safe. Within a minute, I went from hell to heaven. It is because of this experience that I know what it is like. We discussed both the past and the future. He gave many chances for the LTTE to come to a peaceful solution but they didn't accept it, he told me. He asked me to forget the past and told me that they were not the kind of people who would take revenge. He told me I could live comfortably without any worries. We spoke for two hours that day.

From time to time he spoke to me and we also met. Within two to three days he let me speak to my family. I think it was the next day. My wife and daughter were worried but when I called them they were happy and he told me that my family could visit me anytime. Within one or two months my family arrived. I spoke the truth. The war had ended and we had to work for the betterment of the society and the country. A friend of mine told me that I was the only one from the LTTE to win him over. The politicians here have a different image of him. If I have a chance, I'd like to write about these stories.

Sencholai – when we took this land they had already named it Sencholai and we kept the name. Neither the President nor the other officials said anything. This is not for military purposes. There are 140 girls and 40 boys.

Q: After going through all that you went through, how do you introduce yourself?

A: I am a social worker, I am going to devote the rest of my life to society and children. My life should end with these children.

Q: Why did you choose to help children?

A: Elders have completed their life but these children are like flower buds. If they go to the wrong side, the wrong hand, their life will be over. But if you give them a good life and make them independent, they can live a better life. Even after the end of the war, society is messed up. The children are not safe, there's poverty, the girls are leading an unsafe life devoid of parents to care for them. We are looking after 300 girls and they are happy. During the last Government I couldn't do much but now I wish to continue the good work.

Q: What in your view is the biggest mistake you made?

A: I believed the politicians' lies and I missed the life I could have lived. When I was a student I was studious but upon hearing these speeches by various politicians I went over to the other side.

Q: Tell me about your parents?

A: We lived a very difficult life but they wanted to send me a good school as well as university. I did my Bcom at Jaffna University. But at the end of the second year, I was hunted by the Military. I didn't enjoy my life as much at university because I became involved in politics.

Q: When was your first visit to Colombo?

A: In the 1970s by train. Life was different here. People were happy and lived by their culture.

Q: Tell us about your teachers growing up?

A: I remember each of my teachers and both my principals. This college made me different. They were the real teachers. It was never difficult to learn from them, they even came home and taught us.

Q: Why did society deteriorate from what you saw when you were schooling?

A: Certain countries prospered and others were far behind. It was all about the management. Some welcomed the changes and here we took those changes in a different way. They spoiled our country.

Q: You mentioned that you were emotionally influenced by the politicians at your time. Tell us more?

A: Yes, there were several politicians who gave emotional speeches and we were students at the time. They not only misled me, they misled the entire younger generation.

Q: You are a case study of reconciliation, how do you view it?

A: Reconciliation is not an easy task. Many people do not follow it. Every day when the situation or occurrence comes to mind, I compare and analyse it myself. So even from 2009 until now I am with security personnel; sometimes I feel something but I analyse myself and find that they are right. There's no need for me get nervous or worried. I make mistakes but this is a chance they gave me so I accept it. I can't go back. I have to keep my dignity and also prevent others from going back.

Q: Tell us why you chose to teach political science and history?

A: Every person ought to know their history. Children now grow up with little or no proper knowledge of the country's history. They need to know how so many visionaries built this country from the time it gained its independence; it is only if they know that they can help build the country in the same way.

Q: Do you think the current education system fails to teach this?

A: It's all there in the syllabus but there is a lack of teachers. At certain times teachers need to teach particular subjects in-depth but fail to do so. We have struggled all these years because politicians ruled the game but if children are taught what political science is, they can decide what is right and wrong. If they know the country's law, they won't go against the law. But if they are not familiar with the law, they will break the law. When we were younger we broke the law because we felt if the leaders were doing it, we could do it too. Children should acclimatise with the law of the land.

Q: You mentioned you were reading up on biographies. What titles do you recommend?

A: Our country's history, how the kings at the time sacrificed, how they kept the peace. They never compromised the sovereignty of the country for the sake of anything. You see where Japan is today; when the children learn of their country's history, they are very proud of it. We also don't have movies about the lives these kings led and wars they fought. We need to bring this to the younger generation.

Q: When you take your life, you have two eras, one is your involvement with violence and the other one is right after that. You are the best person to understand what reconciliation means and how we should reconcile with each other. Your views?

A: Humanity, who a human is, then you realise that Sinhalese, Tamil, Muslim, Hindu or Buddhist, it is only a symbol, a mark of religion. We have to respect your religion as much as we respect others. If you understand it, you will find that there's no difference among people regardless of their faith. Moreover, if children go to mixed schools, they know they co-exist. Even if we have a bitter experience in the past, we need to forget it and move on. What is the point of these differences, what makes one superior to the other? Nothing. If we had to go to France, we would end up speaking French, so why don't we speak both languages here? It's the politicians here who urged the villagers not to learn Sinhala, but their children are taught both languages in Colombo.

Q: If a kid comes up to you and says they had a dream and want to achieve it, what would you say to them?

A: I will try my best to see that they are able to achieve that dream. I would advise them not to look at the differences of each other, to respect elders and to be ambitious. Nowadays everyone talks about Geneva, but they don't realise how much a Sinhalese mother weeps for her child. They don't realise how many died. It happened on both sides, that is what a war is.

Q: Now that you are in your 60s, how do you see violence, do you realise that it is not a means to achieve anything?

A: Most certainly. The only way we can achieve is through negotiations. Violence can help win a war or two, but how many lives and generations are lost in between?

Q: Since you are well aware of this issue regarding Sri Lanka at the HRC in Geneva, what do you see as being misleading messages regarding Sri Lanka?

A: This will not damage our motherland. This is a tool being used by politicians to show these people that they are working on their behalf. They know very well that both parties made mistakes. It's been 12 years since the end of the war, what's the point of talking about the end of the war?

Q: You mentioned that you were reading about Nelson Mandela and Lee Kuan Yew. What makes them your favourite leaders?

A: How they created their countries. Lee Kuan Yew is Singapore's architect and it is the same for Nelson Mandela for South Africa. I always dream about our President in the same manner. I find him to be a visionary and serious about his aspirations.

Q: You mentioned you had both Sinhala and Muslim students here. Tell us about how you teach them here together?

A: Children are children; they are not taught nor do they see the differences among each other. When they come out to play, their differences disappear.

Q: You also mentioned that you've read a lot about the Dalai Lama and Buddhism, tell us more? What do you find fascinating?

A: I learned about how when you cause harm, you have to also pay the price for it. I always weigh my words and never like to hurt anyone by any means even through words. But it took me over 20 years to learn this. It will not come to you in one day.

Q: What is your dream?

A: I want to see a peaceful, economically developed country where these children have the life they dream of. I'd like to see our people go to Buddhist temples and vice versa. No more mafia, killings and trucks.

Q: What is your responsibility to achieve this?

A: My generation felt it the most because when we were growing up there was no war.

Q: How do you see the war?

A: A game played by a few politicians. Even Prabhakaran misled the youth. When we were young, we were radicalised.

Q: I'd like to know your view about Islamic extremism as we had a bad experience two years ago. How do you see it?

A: We need to look at this seriously. Because believers of Islam are calm and devout people. But someone, people from somewhere, imported terrorism. It is a mistake of the past Government. If our President had been there at that time, it would not have taken place.

Q: What is your message to the critics of this Government?

A: To be patient. Because for over a year the President has been trying to contain the COVID-19 pandemic. But he is also engaged with Tamil politicians. But I am confident that he will deliver on his promise. What I find amusing are the speeches by local Tamil politicians. We call some of them 'puthisali madayan,' which means 'intelligent fool'. They want to keep people under their feet because it is only then that they can control these people.

Q: What is the alternative?

A: It should come naturally, a better, healthier political climate.

Q: Tell me about the Tamil diaspora? Do those living abroad play a responsible role or manipulate the locals here?

A: There are few who are still manipulating but most of them know the truth. In a few years those who are manipulating will give up.

Q: What do you see as being the role of the Tamil intellectuals?

A: They should accept the truth and the reality, then only can they play a role as an intellectual. If they are bent on their views of a separate state, it's in the past and there's no need to talk of it.

Q: When you pray, what do you pray for?

A: A happy and peaceful life for all.

Q: Who are your remarkable students?

A: This girl who is the manager here and another girl at the Jaffna and Batticaloa universities, they are remarkable individuals. They are all special to me. I want to start a school and I want thousands of students to come here and study.

Q: What is your advice to someone who believes that violence is a way to achieve their objective?

A: When you speak to a child, you advise them not to put their finger into the electrical socket or fire, sometimes these people will touch and return because of their experience. With our experience, our country faced very heavy losses, damage, loss of lives, but at the end of the day nothing was achieved. So violence never achieves anything. We can't go forward with violence.

I lost more than half my life to violence. In 2010, I realised my life had gone by. There's no point in crying over it. Even my mother, sister and daughter lost their lives when they travelled by boat to India, I never saw them again. It's my feeling of loss. All of this happened because politicians messed up.

We have now learned from the past. We need to forget about the past and whatever happened in the past. It is our country and we should live happily and support each other. Everyone suffered losses, not just one ethnicity.

ABOUT THE AUTHOR

Nilantha Ilangamuwa is a journalist. He previously served as a Communications Consultant for the Office for National Unity and Reconciliation in the Government of Sri Lanka. A frequent contributor on political affairs, he has written for mainstream local and foreign media, including *Counter Punch*, *Sunday Island*, and *Daily Pioneer*.

Previous Books:

1. *The Conflation*

2. *Lu Xun (Father of Modern Chinese Literature)*